ROBERT PENN WARREN

LITERATURE AND LIFE SERIES
(Formerly Modern Literature and World Dramatists)
GENERAL EDITOR: PHILIP WINSOR

Selected list of titles:

(continued on last page of book)

Robert Penn Warren

Katherine Snipes

FREDERICK UNGAR PUBLISHING CO.
NEW YORK

Grateful acknowledgments to the following:
To Random House Publishing Company for permission to quote
the poem "Sirocco" and excerpts from *Selected Poems 1923–1975,
Brother to Dragons* (Revised Edition), *Now and Then: Poems 1976–
1978, Being Here: Poetry 1977–1980,* and *Rumor Verified: Poems
1979–1980,* all by Robert Penn Warren.

To the librarians of the special Warren collection of the
King Library at the University of Kentucky and their Robert
Penn Warren Oral History Project, a set of taped interviews with
Warren and his friends.

To Steve Oney of *The Atlanta Journal and Constitution
Magazine* for permission to quote from "A Southern Voice."

To Eastern Washington University for helping me with
travel funds and sabbatical leave to examine the Warren
collection at the University of Kentucky.

Library of Congress Cataloging in Publication Data

Snipes, Katherine, 1922–
  Robert Penn Warren.

  (Literature and life series)
  Bibliograpy: p.
  Includes index.
  1. Warren, Robert Penn, 1905–   —Criticism and
interpretation.   I. Title.   II. Series.
PS3545.A748Z867   1983   813′.52   82–40265
ISBN 0–8044–2828–X

Contents

Chronology

April 24, 1905   Born in Guthrie, Kentucky, to Robert Franklin and Anna Ruth Penn Warren
1920   An accident seriously damages one eye and causes Warren to fear sympathetic blindness in the other eye
1921   Enrolls in Vanderbilt University
1924   Becomes a member of the Fugitives
1925   B.A. summa cum laude from Vanderbilt University
1927   M.A. from University of California at Berkeley
1927–1928   Postgraduate work at Yale
1929   Publishes *John Brown: The Making of a Martyr*
1930   Bachelor of Letters, Oxford, as Rhodes scholar
   Publishes "The Briar Patch" in *I'll Take My Stand* by Twelve Southerners, which articulated the stand of the Southern Agrarians
   Marries Emma Brescia
1930–1931   Assistant Professor of English at Southwestern College of Memphis
1931–1934   Acting Assistant Professor of English, Vanderbilt University
1934–1936   Assistant Professor of English, Louisiana State University
   Partnership with Cleanth Brooks, Jr. to produce *Southern Review*
1935   Publishes *Thirty-Six Poems*
1936   Houghton Mifflin Literary Fellowship Award
1936, 1937, and 1938   Carolina Sinkler Prize from the Poetry Society of South Carolina
1936   Publishes, in collaboration with Cleanth Brooks, Jr. and John Thibaut Purser, *An Approach to Literature: A Collection of Prose and Verse* (textbook)
   Levinson Prize from *Poetry Magazine*

1936–1942   Associate Professor of English, Louisiana State University

1936, 1937, and 1940   Member of staff at Writing Conference at University of Colorado

1938   Collaborates with Cleanth Brooks, Jr. for *Understanding Poetry: An Anthology for College Students*

1939–1940   Guggenheim Fellowship

1939   Publishes *Night Rider*

1941   Visiting Lecturer at University of Iowa

1942–1950   Professor of English, University of Minnesota

1942   Publishes *Eleven Poems on the Same Theme*
Shelley Prize for Poetry

1943   Publishes *At Heaven's Gate*
Publishes *Understanding Fiction* in collaboration with Cleanth Brooks

1944   Publishes *Selected Poems*, 1923–1943

1944–1945   Chair of Poetry, Library of Congress

1946   Publishes *All the King's Men*
Publishes "Blackberry Winter," best-known short story

1947–1948   Guggenheim Fellowship

1947   Pulitzer Prize in fiction for *All the King's Men*
National Book Award for *All the King's Men*
Publishes *Circus in the Attic, and Other Stories*

1949   Robert Meltzer Award from Screen Writers' Guild

1950   Columbia Pictures Corporation makes movie of *All the King's Men*, with direction and script by Robert Rossen and Broderick Crawford as Willie Stark
Divorces Emma Brescia Warren
Publishes *Fundamentals of Good Writing: A Handbook of Modern Rhetoric*, in collaboration with Cleanth Brooks (text published in 1949 under title *Modern Rhetoric*)

1

The Sound Reality Makes: Biographical Sketch

The idiot boy who ventures out on pond-ice
Too thin, and hears here—hears there—the creak
And crackling spread. That is the sound Reality

Makes as it gives beneath your metaphysical
Poundage. Memory dies. Or lies.
                                   ("Small Eternity," *Rumor Verified*)

"I think that Robert Penn Warren is the most complete man of letters that we've ever had in this country," says R. W. B. Lewis, who was teaching at Yale University when Warren joined the faculty.[1] Certainly Warren is the only American who has won the Pulitzer Prize for both fiction and poetry: in 1947 for *All the King's Men*, which remains a classic novel of the dynamics of power in rural America; for *Promises: Poems 1954–1956*, a mid-life resurgence of poetic creativity; and in 1979 for *Now and Then: Poems 1976–1978*, a demonstration that his skill in poetry is undiminished in the eighth decade of his life. In collaboration with Cleanth Brooks, Warren has had a tremendous impact on the teaching of literature, since their *Understanding Poetry* and *Understanding Fiction* became the most popular college English texts in the nation. He has written excellent literary criticism, as well as nonfiction of historical and social commentary. In addition, Warren has produced that most rare document, a book-length poetic drama, *Brother to Dragons*, which combines philosophical meditation with a true story of the utmost horror.

1

Robert Penn Warren was born to Robert Franklin and Anna Ruth Penn Warren on April 24, 1905, in Guthrie, a tiny community of 1,200 persons in southwestern Kentucky. His father was a banker—according to Warren, a "misplaced" person—who gave up early aspirations of a literary nature for the more practical aim of making money. Besides caring for young Robert and his brother Thomas and sister Mary, Robert Franklin Warren inherited, at his father's death, a family of small children, the progeny of his father and a young second wife. One does not raise "stacks of children," as Warren puts it, by being a poet.[2]

Although Warren's father, with all his business activities, had little time to spend with his children, he often read to them in the evening—Greek and Roman history and poetry. The parents encouraged the children's intellectual development and the iron rule of discipline was that everyone must do his homework. Warren says his father—a very "un-churchy" man, a freethinker—paid him to read the Bible. "Here's a book you've got to know," he said, ". . . the foundation of society." Warren read it— three times. Father also saw to it, however, that Warren read Darwin's *Origin of Species* before he went to college.

Warren's relationship to his father is a subtle and important one for its impact on his fiction and poetry, which often dramatize father-son relationships. He has a deep admiration for his father's rectitude, especially his humane resolution of the conflicts between personal desires and family duty. This admiration is coupled with a curious feeling of guilt because he, Robert Penn Warren, has lived the literary aspirations that his father gave up. Warren has stated:

"I've always felt guilty about my success as a writer. . . . It's as if I've stolen my father's life. He made his living as a banker, but he started out to be a poet and a lawyer. If he had had the opportunity I did, with his intelligence and energy he'd have done a lot better than I did."[3]

One of Warren's favorite stories recalls the time when he first discovered his father was a poet. When he was twelve years old, he found a hidden book in his book-filled home. It was called *Poets of America* and when he opened it, there was his father's picture with some of his poems. Warren was delighted and brought the book to his father, but the elder Warren simply took the book from him and he never saw it again. Warren thinks his father destroyed it because it reminded him that he had failed to pursue his original goals.

But Warren, who has achieved recognition in so many genres of literature, has never assumed that art is more important than the art of living. In an interview with David Farrell, he speaks nostalgically of the devotion of his parents' "incredible marriage—never a voice raised," and adds meditatively, "ideal but unreal."[4] He is immediately aware that this might be misunderstood, for he hastens to protest the happiness of his own marriage to Eleanor Clark, which does indeed seem unusually fortunate. His first marriage was less than ideal, however, and perhaps he is suggesting that a parental marriage so free from discord is a misleading introduction to the real world. The conflict between idealism and reality and the way a person struggles with disillusionment are among the continuing themes of Warren's fiction. Warren's father, for all his "wasting" his life in business, seems to exemplify for Warren an ideal resolution of one of life's central tasks: to say "yes" to one's own destiny. Personal sacrifice for one's family is not really uncommon, but seldom is it performed without even a trace of bitterness. When his father was an old man, he told Warren serenely that his had been a happy life; he had learned to take joy in his obligations. Warren says sincerely, "I am a very happy man," but adds with a somewhat sad humility, "I can't live up to father's statement about joy in obligation."[5]

"My impression is that I had a happy childhood," Warren says in a newspaper article in the *Lexington Herald*.

But he adds later, with his accustomed recognition that
subjective truth is always ambiguous, perhaps ultimately
unknowable, "Maybe there's some concealed streak of
unhappiness I've never defined."[6] He admits that
Guthrie was a "very un-Southern town—a real estate
man's dreams laid down where two railroad tracks
crossed. I never felt much at home there." Warren also
remembers one terrifying episode at age six when
everyone thought his father was dying. His father was
ordinarily vigorous and healthy, but at age 40 he had
typhoid fever, pneumonia, and gallbladder trouble all at
once. He recovered after an operation, however, and lived
until age 86, when he dropped dead of cancer, having told
no one, not even a doctor, of his affliction.

Warren's summers were spent on his maternal
grandfather's tobacco farm, an environment more suited
to Warren's love of nature. Warren says he collected
"snakes, butterflies, and things" as a child—other lists
include rocks, arrowheads, and leaves. Later, he hunted
with his brother Thomas, and learned to do taxidermy.
He has never lost his early love for the woods, and still
prefers a rural home close to nature. He grumbles that the
woods of Kentucky have been cut down—"looks like
Kansas," he growls. He now spends his summers in the
Vermont woods, where he can hike into the foothills of the
Green Mountains.

He spent one summer, when he was eleven or twelve
in Nashville instead of on his grandfather's farm, but his
activity there was also connected with his naturalist
impulses. He wanted to learn to paint, or more precisely,
he wanted to paint animals. He spent the summer as the
only male pupil in a Catholic academy, where a nun, who
had won first prize in watercolors at the 1893 Chicago
World's Fair, spent patient hours introducing him to that
art. The sisters used to prepare a huge picnic basket so
that Sister Mary Lou and the eager boy artist could spend
the day at Glendale Park, where Warren painted all the

animals in the zoo. He quickly realized, however, that he had no special talent for painting, although he claims he always gets the urge to paint again when he goes to northern California. (Warren's daughter Rosanna is a painter.)

The person of his grandfather was fully as important to Warren's development as the rural setting the grandfather provided. In fact, his grandfather Penn spent more time with the youngster than his father did and figures more prominently in Warren's early poetry. Gabriel Thomas Penn had been a Confederate cavalry-man. He was an ardent reader of military history, an extremely bookish man, and according to Warren, he could quote "poetry by the yard." It is little wonder that Warren has considered the Civil War the great American epic, analogous to the Trojan War for the Greeks. Steve Oney in "A Southern Voice" describes a typical scene of Warren's childhood:

Almost from the time he could walk, Warren spent his afternoons with the old man. Grandpa Penn would sit beneath a tree with the young boy on his knees and reel off ceaseless stories about the Civil War. The grape shot flew, sabres rang. Horses, frothing and blood-streaked, carried their Confederate charges into the din of conflict. Fantasies and fascinations of war whirled through the boy's mind like the fragments of glass in a kaleidoscope. Almost before Warren could read, he knew the power of a story.[7]

This gift of spontaneous storytelling, which may be a regional characteristic of the preindustrial South, is still very typical of Warren's conversation. No matter what topic arises, Warren can spin off a story to illustrate it from the swarming memories of his past. One reason Warren has never had a television is that it would endanger the genial art of tale-telling with friends, which is the treasured heritage of a former time and place. Yet he disdains to write an autobiography and says he could never cooperate patiently with a biographer.

His stories of his own past, like literary art, project
the feeling of a time and place, but they eliminate large
tracts of purely historical fact or deliberately avoid
personal matters that he does not wish to share with the
general public. For instance, he has mentioned in an
interview that his father's bank failed during the
depression, without elaborating upon the impact of that
event on the family. When he meditates upon what the
depression felt like, however, its emotional tone—he
immediately brings forth a little vignette of personal
experience to illustrate a generalization. People during
the depression, he claims, often developed a rare sense of
rapport, of being "all in the same boat," often willing to
share a meager store with those less fortunate. He
illustrates this sensitivity to other people's economic
situation with a story about his brakes failing when he was
driving in the Sierras. After the hair-raising ride (which he
does not elaborate on, since his focus here is on character,
not suspense), he finally comes to a stop on level ground.
An ancient truck stuffed with an old couple and their
grandchildren comes rattling down the road. The old man
stops and asks if he can help. He says he is a wandering
mechanic who helps people who have car trouble on the
road for whatever they can afford to pay. He fixes
Warren's motor in ten or fifteen minutes, replacing a
cotter pin that has worn out. When he finishes and
Warren asks how much he owes, the old man scrutinizes
Warren appraisingly and says, "Two bits; is that too
much, buddy?"[8]

Though Warren had no literary aspirations at all
when he was growing up, he was absorbing the traditional
tales of the South, the characters, the dialects, which
would emerge years later in fiction and poetry. His
brother Thomas, who became a grain dealer and who
claims he doesn't even read books, let alone write them,
nevertheless knew every farmer in five counties and could
swap yarns with them all. Not only stories of the Civil War

and the ever-present folk humor about contemporary events and people, but also accounts of the local tobacco wars, which became the subject of Warren's first novel, *Night Rider*.

In his early years, Warren wanted to become an outdoorsman or an adventurer on the high seas. He might, indeed, have done so, for his father was getting him an appointment at Annapolis—the first step, Warren hoped, to becoming an admiral of the Pacific Fleet. But an unfortunate accident destroyed that dream and prevented his acceptance in any military force thereafter.

When he was fifteen years old, he was lying on the ground behind some bushes. Thomas, several years younger than Robert, was playing on the other side of the bushes and did not know his brother was there. Thomas was tossing rocks into the air. One heavy, sharp-edged stone went over the hedge and smashed down into Robert's eye, damaging it severely. The accident was tragic at the time and for years thereafter, although it may have been crucial to America's gaining a literary artist instead of a naval officer.

The injury affected Warren's psychological state for several years, not just because of the sense of being maimed, but because he feared blindness in the other eye as well. He knew that there was such a thing as sympathetic blindness when the nerve to one eye is damaged. All the time that he was playing the role of carefree college boy at Vanderbilt University, he was secretly testing his eyesight each day for some telltale signs of degeneration. He never told anyone about this or checked with a doctor, even though he was close to suicide during one especially depressed period of 1924. Not until after his graduation, when he was teaching, did he consult a doctor to verify his fears. As a matter of fact, the vision of his good eye was being affected. The damaged eye was immediately removed and replaced by a glass eye, which terminated the tendency to sympathetic blindness. Even this unfortunate obsession had a curious impact upon his intellectual development, for his absorption in reading and writing poetry during his college years was partly a means of escape from his secret fear.

Although the specter of blindness is the factor in his early depression that Warren speaks of freely in interviews for the RPW Oral History Project at the University of Kentucky, to consider this the only factor probably oversimplifies his emotional situation. Marshall Walker's recent book (*RPW: A Vision Earned, 1979*) does not even mention this fear, but does quote a letter from Allen Tate to Donald Davidson concerning Warren's depression (Tate's term is "breakdown"). Tate throws a rather dramatic light upon the matter: "It is simply that he has been beaten down so consistently and brutally, that his emotional needs have met frustration so completely, that he was driven into a blind alley."[9]

Although Tate complains that Dr. Edwin Mims, then head of the English Department at Vanderbilt, does more harm than good with his "solicitude," also termed "nagging," of the young Warren, Tate also says ". . . he [Warren] isn't persecuted by persons, but by hostile ideas, and the persecution is of course a mere figment in the popular mind but very real to an intellectual mind like Red's."[10] Neither Tate nor Mr. Walker in his commentary explain exactly what "hostile ideas" persecuted the sensitive young Warren. One suspects that he rejected some well-meant attempts to convert him; Walker states, "Intellectually he held back from religious orthodoxy ('False tales the saints tell') while his physical unhappiness led him to expect only further misery in a life lived on the naturalistic level."[11] Although the lot of a skeptic among true believers is not a happy one, there were probably other elements in Warren's personal unhappiness at that time. The discrepancies between a naturalistic world and man's religious impulses, however, have haunted Warren's work all his life.

Warren has, of course, a story about his first day at Vanderbilt University. He told it to Steve Oney as they were walking in the Vermont hills. Warren was 74 years old on that occasion.

"I was scared, immature, and totally incompetent to do just about anything. I was a terribly young boy, even younger than my age, which was just sixteen. I was sitting all alone on the steps on one of the buildings there when this massive hand fell across my shoulder with the force of a tumbling chimney. I turned around, saw a grinning, malicious oafish face, and out of that wet mouth came the words: 'Boy, there's only one thing I want to know. Do you ever have evil thoughts?' " Warren parted his lips, flashed his teeth, and brayed laughter.

"The only thing I can be thankful for," he added, "is that he didn't give me any time to answer. He introduced himself, said he was secretary of the YMCA and that he wanted to talk with me about Christ. Said that he'd once partaken of whores, liquor, and cussing—which didn't sound bad to me—but that since he'd been saved, he'd stopped." Warren bunched his cheeks up incredulously. "What's worse, this fellow had taken to turning in bootleggers because he said Christ told him to. God! That was one tough bugger for Jesus. I remember walking by the track one afternoon. He was a track man. He was winding up to throw the discus. He let it fly and then shouted out 'Hey, Red Warren, you're some sort of poet, aren't you? Well, boy, that there was poetry in motion.' "[12]

The really portentous influence of his early college years, however, was that of John Crowe Ransom, who was teaching English composition. Warren had come to college with the intention of majoring in chemical engineering. His interest in chemistry quickly waned, however, in favor of taking more English courses with Ransom. Ransom soon perceived Warren's unusual writing ability and put him in an advanced course, in which he had to imitate the styles of one prominent writer after another. Donald Davidson, who taught sophomore English literature, let Warren write imitations of Beowulf and Chaucer instead of the usual term papers.[13] Warren became fascinated with the poetry of Blake, Keats, Coleridge, and T. S. Eliot, and studied up in secret on Ransom's poetry, too. Ransom's house became almost a second home to Warren, and he started writing poetry under Ransom's direction.

He was not the only talented student to gather at that charmed hour in Nashville, for this was the flowering of the literary group called the Fugitives, which published some of Warren's first verse in the little magazine it produced. According to *The Princeton University Library Chronicle*, "The founders of the Fugitive group were Walter Clyde Curry, Donald Davidson, James M. Frank, Sidney Mittron Hirsch, Stanley Johnson, Merrill Moore, John Crowe Ransom, Alec B. Stevenson, and Allen Tate. Members in absentia were W. Y. Elliott and William Frierson. Jesse and Ridley Wills were added late in 1922, Robert Penn Warren early in 1924, and Laura Riding in March 1925.[14] The magazine they published lasted from 1922 through 1925. Though most contributions were from group members, there were also some outside contributors of note, such as Robert Graves, Louis Untermeyer, and Hart Crane.

The Fugitives were originally a group of townspeople and academics who met regularly to discuss philosophy. By the time Warren entered the group, the focus of attention had shifted somewhat to an examination of poems the members were writing. They had some notion of creating a new Southern literary tradition in opposition to the stereotyped, romantic "magnolia image" of the South in cheap, popular fiction. Their credo was: "The Fugitive flees from nothing faster than the high-caste Brahmins of the Old South." Allen Tate, in an article about the Fugitives, says that

. . . a Fugitive was quite simply a Poet: The Wanderer, or even the Wandering Jew, the Outcast, the man who carries the secret wisdom around the world. It was a fairly heavy responsibility for us to undertake, but we undertook it, with the innocence of which only the amateur spirit is capable.[15]

Warren was the youngest person admitted to the ranks of the Fugitives. Allen Tate has a memorable description of his first meeting with Red Warren:

One day in February 1925 (I think it was) I was typing a bad poem entitled "William Blake" on Walter Clyde Curry's typewriter. Dr. Curry gave the poets the freedom of his rooms. I became aware of a presence at back and turning around I saw the most remarkable looking boy I had ever laid eyes on. He was tall and thin, and when he walked across the room he made a sliding shuffle, as if his bones didn't belong to one another. He had a long quivering nose, large brown eyes, and a long chin—all topped by curly red hair. He spoke in a soft whisper, asking to see my poem; then he showed me one of his own—it was about Hell, and I remember this line:

Where lightly bloom the purple lilies. . . .

He said that he was sixteen years old and a sophomore. This remarkable young man was "Red," Robert Penn Warren, the most gifted person I have ever known.[16]

Red introduced Tate to a friend of his, Ridley Wills, whom Tate characterized as "small, graceful, ebullient, and arrogant, and one of the wittiest and most amusing companions I have ever had."[17] These three extremely bright young men joined up to rent a large room in Wesley Hall, the theological building. (They named the architecture of this edifice Methodist Gothic.) Tate describes their habitation thus:

It was one large room with two double-decker beds, and Ridley and I being older than Red made him sleep above. In order to get into bed at night we had to shovel the books, trousers, shoes, hats, and fruit jars onto the floor, and in the morning, to make walking space, we heaped it all back upon the beds. We stuck pins into Red while he slept to make him wake up and tell us his dreams. Red had made some good black-and-white drawings in the Beardsley style. One day he applied art gum to the dingy plaster and when we came back we saw four murals, all scenes from *The Waste Land*. I remember particularly the rat creeping softly through the vegetation, and the typist putting a record on the gramophone.[18]

After receiving a B.A. summa cum laude from
Vanderbilt in 1925, Warren earned an M.A. from the
University of California at Berkeley. He pronounced
Berkeley "dead" in a literary sense at that time. Having
come from a milieu in which undergraduates in English
often knew "The Waste Land" by heart, it was something
of a disappointment to find that T. S. Eliot had not yet
arrived at Berkeley.

Warren, on the other hand, felt retarded there
because he had not studied Freud or Marx. He was more
or less immune to Marxist revelations because of previous
reading in history. He has later repudiated all one-answer
explanations of historical processes, but at the time he was
protected from Marxist formula by another one, equally
neat, which attributed social development to geography.
His early reading had included Henry Thomas Buckle's
History of Civilization in England, 1870. Buckle says:

If we inquire what those physical agents are by which the human
race is most powerfully influenced, we shall find that they may
be classed under four heads: namely, Climate, Food, Soil, and
the General Aspect of Nature; by which last, I mean those
appearances which, though presented chiefly to the sight, have,
through the medium of that or other senses, directed the
association of ideas, and hence in different countries have given
rise to different habits of national thought.[19]

This still makes considerable sense, especially if, like
Warren, one comes from an area primarily agrarian
rather than industrial. Quite aside from actual background in experience, it suited his naturalistic preferences
in philosophy.

Warren does praise the Elizabethan scholar Willard
Farnham at Berkeley; having been an ardent student of
Elizabethan and Jacobean drama and Renaissance
literature generally, he often taught Elizabethan literature in his later career. He also liked to discuss aesthetics
with philosophy professors Steven Pepper and David
Prall.

After his M.A., Warren started postgraduate work at Yale on a scholarship. That program was interrupted, however, by his being chosen as a Rhodes scholar. He earned a Bachelor of Letters degree at Oxford in 1930.

Meanwhile, Warren had published his first book, not a novel but a historical study—*John Brown: The Making of a Martyr* (1929). He also had his first tantalizing taste of writing fiction, which was really something of an accident. He knew Louis Mumford, Van Wyck Brooks, and Paul Rosenfeld, who ran *The American Caravan*, an annual of more or less modern literature. They had published some of Warren's poems. Rosenfeld cabled to Oxford in Warren's last year there and asked him to write a novelette "like those tales you've told me."[20] The tales concerned the Kentucky tobacco wars, wherein growers banded together to force the tobacco companies to pay decent prices to the grower. Warren proceeded to write his Oxford dissertation in the daytime and his story, "Prime Leaf," at night. Later, he would expand upon the tobacco wars in the novel *Night Rider*.

In 1930 Warren married Emma Brescia, an alliance which was to end in divorce twenty years later. Warren tells no tales about this marriage, either out of a sense of personal privacy or a Southern chivalric view toward women—probably both. His friends are not always so reticent. Some of Warren's associates thought her emotionally unstable, often embarrassing Warren with impulsive behavior in questionable taste. Whatever the problems of this marriage, it probably had some impact on the nature of Warren's creativity. He published three volumes of poetry in 1935, 1942, and 1944. After that there was a long dry period, during which he found he could not finish any poems, although he started many. (He was struggling with his somber, book-length *Brother to Dragons*, written in verse, but was often discontented with that production, too.)

This period was productive enough in terms of prose,

but Warren has felt closer to his poetry and must have grieved for the loss of power in this medium. That it was not just a case of early poetic burnout is demonstrated by the fact that his poetic ability returned with a rush after his marriage to Eleanor Clark and the birth of his first child—a marvelous mid-life renaissance. Moreover, it has never deserted him again.

During his training at Oxford, Warren completed one other writing task that deserves attention. That was his contribution to the Southern Agrarian Manifesto, *I'll Take My Stand: The South and the Agrarian Tradition*, 1930, by Twelve Southerners. The moving spirits of this enterprise are generally conceded to be the four poets Donald Davidson, John Crowe Ransom, Allen Tate, and Robert Penn Warren. Although sometimes criticized as a conservative and unrealistic assessment of the Southern economy, it might also stand as a peculiarly modern criticism of the effects of technology. Lewis B. Rubin, Jr. has assessed the book in this way:

I'll Take My Stand was thus designed as a rebuke to materialism, a corrective to the worship of Progress, a reaffirmation of man's spiritual and aesthetic needs. Neither a treatise on economics, nor a guide to political action, nor yet a sociological blueprint, the Agrarian symposium was an image of what the good life could be.[21]

Warren's contribution to the book was an essay called "The Briar Patch," in which he struggled, perhaps more directly than any of the other writers, with the thorny subject of race relations—the fatal flaw, no doubt, in any idealization of Southern society. He adopted a "separate, but equal" position similar to that of George Washington Carver. It was racist, no doubt, but relatively liberal for its time. Twenty-five years later he completely repudiated his early stand on segregation and conducted a series of interviews with both black and white Southerners, which culminated in the book *Segregation, the Inner Conflict in the*

South, 1956. Still later he interviewed black leaders, including the most radical, and wrote *Who Speaks for the Negro?*

Warren started his teaching career as an assistant professor of English at Southwestern College in Memphis. The next year he returned to his alma mater as acting assistant professor at Vanderbilt, a post he held for three years. In 1934 he moved on to Louisiana State University, where he taught until 1942.

At Louisiana State Warren watched firsthand the political demagogue Huey Long, who provided the germ of the character Willie Stark in *All the King's Men*. Warren protests that Willie Stark is not Huey Long and that he has no idea what Huey Long was really like. What he dealt with was a public myth about Long. Actually Stark could represent any number of public figures who attained to ruthless power with the support of the people.

Warren heard the first of many folk myths about Huey Long from an old hitchhiker he picked up on the road from Tennessee to the University of Louisiana to accept his appointment in 1934. Though he did not recognize it at the time, that old hitchhiker was, for him, a mythological figure—a character who was to appear in *All the King's Men* as the old hitchhiker with a facial twitch, who would lead the cynical Jack Burden to speak of God as the "Great Twitch." Warren elaborates his mythological implications in an essay called "*All the King's Men*: The Matrix of Experience."

He was the god on the battlement, dimly perceived above the darkling tumult and steaming carnage of the political struggle. He was a voice, a portent, and a natural force like the Mississippi River getting set to bust a levee. Long before the Fascist March on Rome, Norman Douglas, meditating on Naples, had predicted that the fetid slums of Europe would make possible the "inspired idiot." His predictive diagnosis of the origins of fascism—and of communism—may be incomplete, but it is certain that the rutted back roads and slab-side shacks that had spawned my nameless old hitchhiker, with the twine-tied paper

parcel in his hand, had, by that fall of 1934, made possible the
rise of "Huey."[22]

Warren lived for years in the midst of a thousand
folk-tales about Huey Long, some of them substantially
true, many imaginary. And the tales, even the most
ungrammatical, were shot through with folk humor,
with philosophy, with hints of violence. Conversations
often dwelt upon questions of power and ethics, of
means and ends, of "historical costs."

Melodrama was the breath of life. There had been melodrama
in the life I had known in Tennessee, but with a difference: in
Tennessee the melodrama seemed to be different from the
stuff of life, something superimposed upon life, but in
Louisiana people lived melodrama, seemed to live, in fact, for
it, for this strange combination of philosophy, humor and
violence. Life was a tale that you happened to be living—and
that "Huey" happened to be living before your eyes. And all
the while I was reading Elizabethan tragedy, Machiavelli,
William James, and American history—and all that I was
reading seemed to come alive, in shadowy distortions and
sudden clarities, in what I saw around me.[23]

These comments illuminate the fact that Warren is
not primarily a historical novelist and certainly not
simply a purveyor of local color. He is a classicist,
interested in the universal qualities of particular experience—a tragedian, more in sympathy with Sophocles
and Shakespeare and Melville than with Bret Harte. It
also illustrates Warren's tendency to let the material for
a novel lie fallow in his memory for a long time before it
emerges at last as art. He can almost always describe
the moment when the seed for a story, or even a poem,
dropped into his consciousness. But the plant is always
nurtured for a long time in the hothouse of the psyche
before it is presented to the world. Whatever it had of
topicality or historical fact is subordinated to the
universal myth or the imaginative construct. That is
why *All the King's Men*, which won the Pulitzer Prize for

fiction in 1947, can outlast the topical notoriety of the historical Huey Long.

Warren writes ironically that although Louisiana was "Huey's University," Long never interfered with the classroom. "The only time that his presence was ever felt in my classroom was when, in my Shakespeare course, I gave my little annual lecture on the political background of *Julius Caesar*: and then, for the two weeks we spent on the play, backs grew straighter, eyes grew brighter, notes were taken, and the girls stopped knitting in class, or repairing their faces."[24] Warren points out that myth and historical reality became one at that moment in September 1935 when Huey Long met his Brutus in the corridor of the Louisiana state capitol and dropped from an assassin's bullets.

At Louisiana State, Warren began his association with Cleanth Brooks, Jr., one of the most genial and fruitful partnerships in American letters. He and Brooks cooperated first to create and edit the literary magazine, *Southern Review*. John Lewis Longley has called the *Southern Review*, "during its brief lifetime perhaps the most distinguished literary quarterly in the world."[25] But their most lasting contributions to the profession of teaching were the textbooks *An Approach to Literature* (with John Thibaut Purser, 1936), *Understanding Poetry* (1938), and *Understanding Fiction* (1943). These did more than anything else to propagate what has been called the New Criticism, a much misunderstood term.

At the 1979 College English Association meeting, Cleanth Brooks addressed the group on "Forty Years of Understanding Poetry," providing a short history of the production of their most famous textbook and seeking to correct some misconceptions about their intentions. Brooks explains the situation at Louisiana thus:

. . . Warren and I found ourselves in the mid-1930's teaching at Louisiana State University. We had overlapped a year at

Vanderbilt in the 1920's and later we had overlapped a year at Oxford. Now in 1934 we had come together again. Among other things, each of us was teaching a section of the department's course in literary forms and types. Granted that Warren and I were young men excited by the new trends in literature—were full of literary theory drawn from the poetry and critical essays of T. S. Eliot and from the then sensational books on theory and practical criticism written by I. A. Richards—nevertheless, our dominant motive was not to implant newfangled ideas in the innocent Louisiana sophomores we faced three times a week. Our motive was to try to solve a serious practical problem.[26]

That practical problem was one which most college English teachers still face. Students approach a poem, Brooks points out, as they would an advertisement in a Sears-Roebuck catalog. "The purpose of all discourse was to convey information and to deliver it straight. All must be rendered as plain as a pikestaff."[27] No one had ever demonstrated to his or her students how a poem works. And the anthologies in use at the time did not provide much help in the understanding of metaphorical language, the nature of irony, the mysteries of symbol, the functions of imagery and rhythm. Brooks says that the notes in the current texts, if any at all were provided, gave meanings of difficult words or allusions or historical and biographical facts. Brooks and Warren certainly had no objections to these features, but the students needed more. A poem might be introduced by "a bit of impressionistic criticism, such as praise for the ravishing beauty of the poet's evocation of an English garden in mid-May. . . ." This provides very little aid to students of limited reading experience.

The first "book" was simply a set of mimeographed class notes, much of it Warren's, to distribute to their literature classes. Brooks describes this auspicious event thus:

The little booklet of some thirty pages was then mimeographed and we distributed copies to our students. A little later, we decided to do a full-dress book that would provide a text for teaching poetry, fiction, drama, and essays. The book was written, and brought out by the LSU Press in 1936. It was entitled *An Approach to Literature*. I must add that it was not received by the English Department with deafening cheers. It clearly cut across the grain of our colleagues' tastes and past training. Some of our comments on particular stories and poems aroused downright outrage. As I now realize, we must have appeared to be two very brash and bumptious young men who, from our Oxford experience, had got well above our rearing. I quickly learned that *An Approach to Literature* was sometimes referred to in the department as *The Reproach to Literature*, a witticism that Warren and I began to use ourselves when one of us mentioned the book to the other.[28]

The text thus produced got a wider audience because Mr. Fred Crofts persuaded the writers and the LSU Press that a university press does not have the facilities to publish a textbook. Crofts took it over to his "small and rather choosy" textbook company. At that time, the company bore the name of Crofts alone, but it later merged with other publishing houses to become Appleton-Century-Crofts.

Thus, out of practical need to benefit uninstructed readers, who could understand only the plainest expository prose, was born the main vehicles for the so-called New Criticism. It was really an extension of those many midnight sessions of the Fugitives at Vanderbilt—a close examination of the art object to see what makes it work.

The opposition to the methods of Brooks and Warren arose mostly from what they left out of the discussion. As Brooks expresses it, ". . . the principal charge was that Warren and I meant to eliminate from the study of poetry all reference to history, biography, and cultural background."[29] This was *not* their intention. It would be absurd to assume that Warren, to whom history and cultural milieu are so important, would be uninterested in such literary influences. Brooks and Warren were simply supplementing literary study where it seemed weakest. Brooks explains the weakness thus:

. . . The graduate school discipline which had molded the typical instructor of the 1930's stressed background, cultural climate, biography, and history. It was long on these items but very short on the study of the poem as work of art. This was the general situation in my own graduate school experience and I take it to have been also in Warren's. So in *Understanding Poetry* we were simply applying the grease to the wheel that squeaked worst. We expected the *instructor* to supply biographical and historical data, for we took it for granted that he was at least equipped to do that. In our limited space, in a book of small compass, we would try to supply something else—something that evidently wasn't being supplied by the current textbooks and apparently wasn't a part of the repertoire of the average instructor.[30]

Brooks and Warren became the targets for a lively, sometimes rancorous academic debate, but, generally speaking, their pedagogical method swept over America with considerable success. Brooks quotes Hazard Adams in *The Interests of Criticism* for an account of what happened from 1938 to 1958. Adams explains some of the misconceptions thus:

The New Critics were not, as many of the cultural historians seemed to think, trying to separate literature from life. Their view was that philological and historical scholarship had made literature disappear by converting it into linguistic specimen or historical document. The critic should read literature as if it were an art. This meant literature had to be distinguished from other modes of statement conceptual in nature and subject to rational standards or proof. The New Critics held that poetry was a mode of language with its own unique cultural value; it returned man from the abstraction of intellect to a contemplation of the particulars and complexities of individual experience.[31]

If the New Criticism is now losing some of its vogue in academia, it is for a reason ironically analagous to its beginning at Louisiana State. The scales may have tipped too far the other way. Now, it is becoming daring or different to investigate the historical or sociological or psychological relevance of literature. Meanwhile, the need for guidance in the understanding of literature remains constant while teachers continue to face students who approach poetry with skills suitable for reading the Sears-Roebuck catalog.

In 1942 Warren moved to the University of Minnesota as a full professor of English. He had published *Night Rider* by then and was working on his second volume of poems. He had already received several poetry prizes and literary fellowships. The novel *At Heaven's Gate* came out the next year as did the third textbook with Brooks, *Understanding Fiction*. In later years Brooks and Warren collaborated further with textbooks in rhetoric.

Warren took time out from teaching in 1944–1945, when he became the poetry consultant for the Library of Congress and edited the *Library Quarterly*. It was there that his friend Katherine Anne Porter, who occupied the chair for fiction, threw on his desk a document she had found in the archives. "This is for you," she said. "I'm giving you a novel."[32] It was the confession of one Jeroboam Beauchamp, who had been hanged for murder in Kentucky in 1826. This was the genesis of *World Enough and Time, A Romantic Novel*, which would simmer in Warren's mind until 1950.

Warren reports, with some amusement, that all during World War II the library was using Japanese tissues to repair the cracks in documents such as the Declaration of Independence and the Constitution. Someone objected to "enemy" material used in this intimate way on our sacred documents. Since the library had an ample supply of Japanese tissues and these were still the best for repairing old manuscripts, Warren solved the problem linguistically by designating such tissues thereafter as "an appropriate substance."[33]

The same year that *All the King's Men* came out (1946), Warren published his best-known short story,

"Blackberry Winter," drawing heavily upon his own childhood. He went on to produce a volume of short stories, *The Circus in the Attic, and Other Stories* (1947). After this interlude with the short-story genre, however, Warren gave up this literary form altogether. He said short stories kill poems. This was during that period, mentioned earlier, when his poetry repeatedly aborted.

During this rather difficult period, however, an altogether new art form was struggling for expression. In the Library of Congress he had pored over old newspapers and abolitionist literature that dealt with a gory Kentucky folktale. It was an incredible but true story in which a man chopped a young Negro slave to pieces with a meat ax, before the terrified eyes of his other slaves. The ironic twist to this horror story was that the perpetrator of the deed and his younger brother, who witnessed it, were sons of the sister of Thomas Jefferson, writer of the Declaration of Independence. The tragic irony of Jefferson, believer in the goodness and perfectibility of man, having to acknowledge such fiendish behavior in his own family fascinated Warren, who has an almost Calvinistic view of man's corruptibility. Around this dismal event, Warren constructed a complex book-length poem, which combines drama with philosophical contemplation.

Brother to Dragons: A Tale in Verse and Voices (1953), like *All the King's Men*, was written in several forms before its present one. Moreover, Warren was never entirely satisfied with it and recently revised the poem again (1979). It has been performed as drama in Texas, Seattle, New York, Providence, and Boston. There was also a television production, which Warren says was "rotten." Warren played his own father in that production; he was surprised on viewing the film that he had, quite unconsciously, reproduced the gestures his father used to make. When he was writing *Brother to Dragons*, Warren admitted to his friend, Joseph Warren Beach, head of the English department at Minnesota, that he had just begun to understand his father.[35]

All the King's Men was written first as a verse play (produced sixty to seventy-five times, Warren says) and then as a prose play, first produced by Irwin Pisiotor at the President Theatre in New York City in 1947. There the Dramatist Play Service published it. It has been performed many times, both in the United States and in Germany, Poland, and the Soviet Union. Warren says it ran for two years in Moscow.[36] He received the Robert Meltzer Award from the Screen Writers' Guild, as well as the Pulitzer Prize for fiction for the novel. It has been translated into twenty languages. In 1981, Harold Prince directed a musical based on it, "William Stark," which premiered at Houston's Jones Hall and Washington's Kennedy Center. Carlisle Floyd composed the score and the baritone Timothy Nolen played Stark.

With these accomplishments in dramatic art, Warren became professor of playwriting at Yale University in 1951. He quit Yale several times but kept returning from time to time, sometimes for limited appointments, one term a year. He has always liked teaching, especially the stimulating contact with colleagues, and he has known many of the most prominent scholars, writers, and teachers in America. And he enjoys talking about literature with young people. He thought he was leaving Yale for good in 1956 to tend to his writing and editing, but he returned in 1961 as professor of English, until he finally retired as professor emeritus in 1973.

In 1952, a year or so after Warren divorced his first wife, he married the writer Eleanor Clark. Clark had written one novel, *The Bitter Box*; during their marriage she has raised two children and produced several books of fiction and nonfiction, receiving the National Book Award in 1965 for *The Oysters of Locmariaquer*. Warren and his wife still part company each morning, each retiring to his or her own private nook to spend several uninterrupted hours in writing.

Not every man pushing fifty cares to start a family, but there has seldom been a more enchanted middle-aged father than Warren. He even delivered his first child himself—not through prior planning, to be sure, but because Rosanna insisted upon making her appearance rather suddenly one evening in the Warren living room. They were living at a considerable distance from any hospital. He and Eleanor also have a second child, a boy, Gabriel Penn; Red told his friends, Bill [Professor William Van O'Connor] and Mary O'Connor, that he would have added Tilimicus, a family name, if he had dared.[37]

The literary impact of his personal situation as husband and father was striking, to say the least. What emerged from the poetically reawakened psyche was *Promises: Poems 1954–1956*, which won the National Book Award for poetry, the Edna St. Vincent Millay Prize from the Poetry Society of America, and the Pulitzer Prize for poetry. His poetic voice has never left him; he won the coveted Bollingen Prize in poetry in 1967 and a second Pulitzer Prize for poetry in 1969 and continues to write both poetry and fiction. He was awarded the National Medal for literature in 1970.

With *Promises*, the persona of Warren's poetry becomes practically identical with himself. He is speaking of his own experience, his own past, his own children (the promise of the future), his own meditations on the mystery of time and the meaning of personal identity, which he has explored for so long in fiction and folklore. The romantic setting for the writing of *Promises* is a ruined fortress where he and Eleanor lived in Italy—Cesare Borgia's hunting ground, says Warren, who always knows his history— "those blood-soaked stones." Rosanna was one year old, providing a contrast to the grim past.

> To a place of ruined stone we brought you, and sea-reaches.
> *Rocca*: fortress, hawk-heel, lion-paw, clamped on a hill.
> A hill, no. On a sea cliff, and crag-cocked, the embrasures
>   commanding the beaches,

Range easy, with most fastidious mathematic and skill.

Philipus me fecit: he of Spain, the black-browed, the
    anguished,
For whom nothing prospered, though he loved God.
His arms, a great scutcheon of stone, once over the
    drawbridge
                                        have languished
Now long in the moat, under garbage; at moat-brink,
    rosemary
            with blue, thistle with gold bloom, nod.

Sun blaze and cloud tatter, now the sirocco, the dust swirl
    is swirled
Over the bay face, mounts air like gold gauze whirled; it
    traverses
                        the blaze-blue water.
We have brought you where geometry of a military rigor
    survives
                            its own ruined world,
And sun regilds your gilt hair in the midst of your
    laughter.[38]

Is it the geometry of the ruined Renaissance world of
which he sings or the ruined world of the South —
Grandpa Penn's South—which Warren imagined in his
own innocent childhood? Of course, all worlds are or will
be fallen—that is why innocence seems such a miracle.

In the last several years misfortune has fallen on the
Warren household. Eleanor was stricken with a destructive eye disease called macular degeneration. The doctors
thought she was going completely blind. The disease
stabilized after six months, however, leaving her vision
extremely dim and blurred. Nevertheless, she began to
write again, using magic markers on huge sheets of
newsprint, transcribing her notes onto a large-print
typewriter fitted with a powerful magnifying glass. She
wrote *Eyes, Etc. A Memoir* about her struggle with the
affliction—no fruitless wailing or sentimentality, but a
hard look at humanity's common lot.[39] She correlates it

somewhat with Homer's perception of suffering in the
Iliad, which Warren was reading to her in the evenings.
They had decided to revisit the great works of western
literature together, one after another.

Eleanor has learned to live with her handicap by
ordering her house precisely and memorizing where
everything is. She still writes, still cooks, still entertains
friends, and still battles verbally with Warren on all kinds
of intellectual issues, for she is a Connecticut Yankee,
formerly a Trotskyite,[40] a stimulating match for a former
Southern Agrarian. As she wrote in *Eyes, Etc.*, ". . . it's
what's made of time that lets us out of it without loss of
life."[41]

What will Warren do next? Who knows? Some
friends wonder if he might produce a novel based on his
relationship to his father. Mary O'Connor points out that
the search for a father is not just a cliché devised by
literary critics; it is often a psychological reality for
writers.[42] Warren has written considerable poetry about
his father in recent years. Almost certainly, more poetry
will appear. In "Afterthought," at the end of *Being Here:
Poetry 1977–1980*, Warren says, ". . . fiction may be more
deeply significant than fact. Indeed, it may be said that
our lives are our supreme fiction."

There is a critical reason, quite aside from general
interest in a colorful personality, for dwelling at some
length upon Warren's personal life and cultural milieu.
Considering his close association with the New Criticism,
it is perhaps ironic that Warren's work invites other
approaches. We have already noted that the effect, though
not the intent, of the New Criticism's approach was to
promote close examination of the art object to the
exclusion of extrinsic matters such as biographical facts or
sociological situations. Warren himself does not exclude
such information in writing criticism, nor is it appropriate
in considering Warren's poetry and fiction. In fact, for one
so steeped in cultural myths and so engrossed in his own

reenactment of—or attempts to escape from—mythic patterns, extrinisic factors are particularly relevant.

One appropriate approach to Warren's writing is that described by Leslie Fiedler in his article "Archetype and Signature."[43] Fiedler uses the term *archetype* rather than *myth* because of the increasingly fuzzy meaning of the latter term. He means "any of the immemorial patterns of response to the human situation in its most permanent aspects: death, love, the biological family, the relationship with the Unknown, etc., whether those patterns be considered to reside in the Jungian Collective Unconscious or the Platonic World of Ideas."[44] These, whatever their origin, belong to the "Community at its deepest, pre-conscious levels of acceptance." By *signature* Fiedler means "the sum total of individuating factors in a work, the sign of the Persona or Personality through which an Archetype is rendered, and which itself tends to become a subject as well as a means of the poem."[45] As Fiedler suggests, literature is born when signature is imposed on archetype. One more quotation from Fiedler's article supports my occasional observations on the relationship between Warren's art and his private experience:

The poet's life is the focusing glass through which pass the determinants of the shape of his work: the tradition available to him, his understanding of "kinds," the impact of special experiences (travel, love, etc.). But the poet's life is more than a burning glass; with his work, it makes up his total meaning. I do not intend to say, of course, that some meanings of art, satisfactory and as far as they go sufficient, are not available in the single work itself . . . ; but a whole body of work will contain larger meanings, and where it is available, a sense of the life of the writer will raise that meaning to a still higher power. The latter two kinds of meaning fade into each other; for as soon as two works by a single author are considered, side by side, one has begun to deal with biography—that is, with an interconnectedness fully explicable only in terms of a personality, inferred or discovered.[46]

2

Living in Time:
Explorations, 1923–1943

> We live in time so little time
> And we learn all so painfully, . . .
> —"Bearded Oaks"

The search for identity, Warren's major theme, has become such a cliché that anyone who has explored this theme seriously may now risk only superficial attention. That is unfortunate, since the issue is still a very real one in a time of rootlessness and disintegrating traditions. Warren is one of the most academic and learned of our writers, steeped in traditional literature, history, and even subliterary writings (journals, confessions, etc.), pertinent to American history. He knows, better than most, how America has changed and what this change has cost. Warren is both a classicist, concerned with discovering universal truths about human life, and a very personal artist, endlessly exploring his own microcosmic experience, his own struggle to identify himself in relation to his family origins, to the Southern tradition, to modern technological society, and to nature. One is tempted to add "God," but to Warren God seems quite alien to the traditional deity—a convenient metaphor, nevertheless, for the mysterious order of the cosmos.

Warren is a poet—first, last, and best. Perhaps if he were "only" a poet, he would be widely recognized as one of the best America has produced. His versatility has actually blurred his impact upon those who would judge

him. Few academics whom I know personally have read
much of his poetry, although they are all familiar with
his famous novel, *All the King's Men*, and many have
studied *Understanding Poetry* and *Understanding Fiction*. The
last nonacademic reader I spoke to about Warren said,
"Oh, he writes pornographic novels, doesn't he? I read
something recently which was mostly about sex." The
last comment derives, I suppose, from Warren's latest
novel, *A Place to Come To*, but the reader could not
remember the name. Fortunately, Warren is not as much
concerned about his public image as about his personal
identity.

That struggle to understand and express his own
private experience colors much, perhaps all, of Warren's
writing, even when he is exploring a historical event,
constructing a modern novel, or explicating other writers' works. To read Warren on Melville or Coleridge or
Hawthorne, for instance, provides insight into Warren
himself. This is not intended to deprecate Warren's
critical perception or to suggest that he is especially self-
centered. Quite the contrary. It suggests that literature
can be best understood and interpreted by persons of like
mind and training who are concerned about similar
human questions. Warren does not despise well-traveled
roads any more than Sophocles, Dante, or Shakespeare
did. The following passage about Hawthorne comes from
some undated notes in the Warren papers in the King
Library (University of Kentucky). It could be written
about Warren as well as about Hawthorne and be just as
valid.

He lived in the right ratio—right for the fueling of his genius—
between an attachment to his region, and country, and a cold
assessment of it, between attraction to the past and repudiation
of the past, between attraction to the world and contempt for its
gifts, between a powerful attraction to women and a sexual
flinch, between a faith in life and corrosive skepticism, between
a capacity for affection and an innate coldness, between a

fascinated attentiveness to the realistic texture, forms, and characteristics of nature and human nature, and a compulsive flight from that welter of life toward abstract ideas, and between, most crucial of all, a deep knowledge of self and an ignorance of himself cultivated in a fear of the potentialities of self.

Having presented this summary of paradoxical tensions in Hawthorne, every one of which could be applied to Warren's poetry and fiction, we nevertheless approach his complex literary career in the easiest way—chronologically. Although his thematic interests are quite constant throughout his life, they are expressed somewhat differently at different states of his development. There is a significant break in poetry production around 1943, followed by a prose period, then a spectacular resumption of poetry, with continued creativity in both poetry and fiction thereafter.

Warren tried his hand at all the major genres of literature in those first twenty years from 1923 to 1943, which is the span designated by his third book of poetry, *Selected Poems*. In that time he wrote his first long story, "Prime Leaf," his first "historical" novel (actually based on stories heard as a child), and a modern novel, as well as collaborating with Cleanth Brooks on successful textbooks. In poetry, he began emulating the great metaphysical poetry of Donne and Marvel, but he soon developed his own idiom and style and created a unique, balladlike folk narrative punctuated by philosophical comment. Although he did not publish any drama during this period, he wrote plays that were produced a number of years later.

John Brown: The Making of a Martyr (1929)

His first book, however, was none of these, but a history of John Brown, written with a distinctly Southern perception of that fanatic abolitionist. *John Brown: The Making of a Martyr (1929)*, is more notable as a practice ground for

Warren's fiction than as entirely dependable history. According to Leonard Casper, the biography of Brown was one of several historical studies by the Vanderbilt group to counteract the exclusively Northern bias of contemporary histories. Allen Tate, for instance, wrote studies of Stonewall Jackson, Jefferson Davis, and Robert E. Lee. Actually, such investigations were often too critical and honest for the tastes of more sentimental Southerners.[1] One might as well admit that all historical writing is, to some extent, biased, always dependent upon a particular person's choice of details and manner of presentation.

In Warren's case, at least, the effect is rather like reading about the Revolutionary War from the British point of view. This is not to say that Warren was dishonest in the account or that he tampered with known facts. He even admits that the sources sometimes offer conflicting stories of the same event. But where evidence is meager or contradictory, he imposes upon it his own interpretation. And he often resorts to purely fictional techniques of reporting the private thoughts and motivations of John Brown without citing the sources that led him to such assumptions.

John Brown acquires, therefore, a partly fictional character, which may or may not reflect his true personality. Note the elaboration on fact in the following description of Brown's entrance into a Kansas town supportive of Free State views:

. . . The shout rose up for him, for the hero, for Osawatomie Brown. He took no apparent pleasure in them, as he rode slowly, abstractedly, through the crowd, for he was not the man to show the concession of pleasure when he only received what he felt to be a just reward of his worth. In the times when there were no cheers, his pride and egotism had fed on a great secret reserve of certainty and self-approbation; in short, they had fed on themselves, and fattened. But the applause of other people, the strict and forced obedience of his own family and followers, the cringing, half-fearful devotion of the fine sheep-dog he had shot when it followed another man were all necessary to him; they filled a profound need and supported him, but they gave no pleasure. . . .

Brown has already been revealed as an opportunist, a land speculator, a failed businessman, and a cold-blooded murderer. He may, indeed, have been all of these, but the young Warren was creating a self-serving villain, who is clearly akin to later fictional characters: Professor Ball, Dr. MacDonald, and Mr. Munn of *Night Rider*, Bogan Murdock of *At Heaven's Gate*, and even Willie Stark of *All the King's Men*.

Warren also expresses in this biography his antipathy to Ralph Waldo Emerson as a dealer in empty words, with little perception of the real world. Henry David Thoreau once had both Emerson and Brown to dinner. Warren quotes Emerson as saying, "He [Brown] is a man to make friends wherever on earth courage and integrity are esteemed—the rarest of heroes, a pure idealist, with no by-ends of his own." Warren obviously does not believe Brown was a "pure idealist"; moreover, Warren has a continuing distrust of "pure idealists," whoever they may be. One wonders if Warren's long-standing antipathy to Emerson, however, is perhaps colored by Emerson's lionizing of John Brown as a noble abolitionist. In fiction, Warren is inclined to show abstract idealists as lacking in self-knowledge, capable of self-righteous violence because they refuse to acknowledge their own irrational impulses. The best example of this personality type in Warren's fiction is Adam Stanton in *All the King's Men*, who assassinates Willie Stark for seducing Adam's sister.

One of Warren's central intuitions about human life is that strong-willed people seek to define themselves in action. Although obsessive self-assertion may disguise itself as exalted idealism, it is secretly fed by a fear of nothingness, a sense of hollowness at the core of one's being. Thus, Warren interprets John Brown's refusal to accept insanity as the only viable defense in his trial for treason, conspiracy, and murder after his attack on Harpers Ferry:

... It would have meant a repudiation of himself, and in comparison to such a thing the danger of the noose was inconsequential; it would have meant that he himself was nothing, and all his life, since the youthful period of doubt when he felt a "steady, strong desire to die," had been spent in a ruthless, passionate attempt to prove to the world that he, John Brown, was something.

This may indeed be an accurate perception of John Brown, but we cannot know this. Warren's interpretation has the virtue of plausibility, a necessity for fiction, and is characteristic of a number of his fictional characters.

Night Rider (1939)

There is a great void in the self which wants to be filled with something greater than itself, which is the attraction of "missions," of the impulse to martyrdom, of leadership in a cause. This is what Warren found in the history of John Brown and this is what he dramatizes in his first novel, *Night Rider*. As John Brown resorts to pillage and murder in the name of abolishing slavery, Mr. Perse Munn, protagonist of *Night Rider*, resorts to pillage and murder in the name of defending tobacco growers against the monopolistic tyranny of the tobacco company. What begins as a legitimate cooperative among growers against unscrupulous capitalists ends as a lawless band, much like the Ku Klux Klan, taking the law into its own hands. The rebellion against tyranny becomes, as it so often does in real life, a new form of tyranny.

The focus of the story is the impact of these events upon the young lawyer, Mr. Munn, who, like tragic heroes generally, does not know himself. He seems at first a rather passive, ordinary, conventional man, with all unlawful tendencies thoroughly repressed. Because of this ignorance of his own proclivities, he is quite easily manipulated by other more forceful and knowledgeable people. His friend, Mr. Christian, who is almost pure dynamism, the man of passion and action, exercises a nearly irresistible attraction. It is Christian who first draws Mr. Munn into the Association of Growers of Dark Fired Tobacco.

What begins as a rather simple appeal to a young lawyer's vanity and sense of social justice gradually develops into a more sinister temptation to deeds of a darker nature. It is not enough to persuade growers to join the boycott; there are always some who will not cooperate. Two outsiders, who are theorizers and organizers, arrive on the scene—Professor Ball and his son-in-law Dr. MacDonald. These advocate a secret society within the association, which will "scrape" the fields, destroying the new tobacco plants, of those who refused to join the strike. Mr. Munn, at first repudiating such unlawful methods, is nevertheless persuaded by the seemingly rational arguments and by something in his own nature that he has not yet recognized. There are distinct overtones of a pact with the devil, although readers may not catch the implications. Professor Ball is described in vaguely ominous terms: he spits, for instance, with a "quick, viper-like forward thrust of the long neck." Munn's first duty as a member is to write a list of men who might join the Night Riders. There is some problem with getting the ink to flow in the pen; the only function of this detail must be to suggest Dr. Faustus's difficulty in getting his blood to flow freely when he must sign his pact with Mephistopheles.

The next step in Mr. Munn's road to perdition is also just a logical development from the initial situation. Bunk Trevelyon, whom Mr. Munn once defended successfully against a charge of murder, betrays his sacred oath to the Night Riders and sells out to the enemy. The group decides that it cannot let backsliders go unpunished. The punishment for betrayal must be death. And when the lots are cast, Mr. Munn wins the role of leader of the avengers.

Thus, the cause of justice leads to premeditated murder, which for Munn is the climax of his recognition of the dark side of his own nature. For he knows now that the killing of Trevelyon is not just his duty to the group; it satisfies something very personal for himself. He realizes at last what he had sometimes guessed but tried to repress: that Trevelyon had committed the murder of which he was once accused and that the Negro who was hanged for that murder was innocent. Trevelyon thus becomes the symbol for Munn's half-conscious cooperation in framing the Negro. In this ritual of retribution, the shared myth of community justice fuses with Munn's private myth of killing the shadow-self—an act both of self-condemnation and deliberate concealment of secret crime.

There is one step beyond this stage of the economic war, but by this time Mr. Munn, like the fallen Macbeth, no longer makes moral objections. Professor Ball and Dr. MacDonald, with the willing cooperation of Mr. Munn, lead a concerted assault on the company warehouses. The goal is to destroy the tobacco supply that the companies have managed to accumulate in spite of the general boycott. Of course, in so complicated a maneuver there are some casualties. One person who dies is young Benton Todd, who has been an ardent admirer of Munn and relatively naïve concerning the ethics of the leaders. Moreover, the young man had hoped to marry Christian's daughter, who is having a secret affair with Munn. If Trevelyon symbolizes the murderous shadow-self that Mr. Munn has hated to acknowledge, Benton Todd suggests the lost idealism, the better self that Munn has betrayed.

Mr. Munn eventually becomes a fugitive, accused of a murder he did not commit—the silencing of one of the members who had agreed to turn state's evidence against

Dr. MacDonald. After a long, somewhat blank period when a poor farmer shelters Munn, he [Munn] returns to murder a former senator, named Tolliver, who had first flattered him into thinking he had an important political career ahead of him and later betrayed the association that trusted him. This project seems to have no meaning for Munn other than to fill that vacancy of the self. He does not kill Tolliver, however, partly because he perceives that the wretched man is just as empty as himself and would welcome death. Mr. Munn is shot down by soldiers outside Tolliver's house.

In one sense, the later part of the novel, which follows the gripping narrative of the burning of the company warehouses, is somewhat anticlimatic—a tying up of loose ends. Its one redeeming feature, however, is a set piece that acts as a contrast to the story of Mr. Munn's downfall. Proudfit, the impoverished farmer who is sheltering Munn, tells of his own checkered career in the West as a buffalo hunter and hide tanner, with companions as rough and wild as he himself. Eventually, however, he lived in peace among Indians. When he fell deadly sick, the Indians cared for him, using all their resources of natural healing and religious ritual. In his fever, he eventually had a vision of Kentucky, where he was raised, and of a young woman waiting beside a stream. His strength then began to return, and he left his Indian friends and came back to find the very woman he saw in his vision, who is now his wife, and the very hill he saw, which is now his farm.

Proudfit's story is both an engrossing dialect narrative and a unique version of the underlying myth of death and resurrection. Proudfit's humble redemption contrasts with the myth of sin and damnation implied in Munn's career. Both Proudfit and Munn have a period of withdrawal (Proudfit among the Indians, Munn on Proudfit's remote farm), with time to rethink their past lives and future goals. This experience is analogous to the withdrawal and contemplation that the mythic hero undergoes before he returns to his homeland as a new person. Munn, however, is not transformed. He does become mildly obsessed with the Negro who died in Trevelyon's stead, but he cannot even remember the man's name. Perhaps his inability to name the scapegoat is intended to suggest Munn's distance from the redemption offered by Christ's sacrifice. I do not mean that Warren is pushing Christianity, as some of his more pious associates at Vanderbilt did. But he is admitting, perhaps, the existence of a moral vacuum where traditional values have been eliminated in a society concerned primarily with status and wealth.

Several motifs first developed in *Night Rider* reappear periodically in Warren's fiction. The symbiotic relationship between active and passive personalities, here represented by Christian and Munn, will attain its most complex elaboration in the relationship between Stark and Burden in *All the King's Men*. Unlike Burden, however, Munn changes from a passive role to a more active one and seems more clearly related to the literary tradition of tragedy. He is sometimes likened to Macbeth, who, according to his indomitable wife, was too full of the milk of human kindness to catch the nearest way. Macbeth gained in ambition and ruthlessness as his wife lost that strength, which at first exceeded his.

At Heaven's Gate will provide an even better example of the secondary plot told in dialect by a poor, unsophisticated narrator. Like Proudfit's story, the tale of Ashley Windham will be a poor man's spiritual quest for redemption. So also the story of Cass Mastern, which puzzles Jack Burden. And Warren's protagonists, whether the political manipulators of the city or the simple farmers and preachers of the rural areas, will continue to follow the patterns of myth, involving the fall from innocence, the confrontation with the shadow-self, the symbolic journey westward, and the return, sometimes to new life, but often to death or devastating self-knowledge.

Night Rider is, in some ways, one of Warren's best novels because of its relatively uncluttered impact as tragedy. *All the King's Men* is better controlled, largely through point of view; *World Enough and Time* is undoubtedly a more profound and complex treatment of human error. But the moral issues in *Night Rider* are sharper and clearer, perhaps because Warren's developing imagination and insight had not yet realized the full complexity of social relationships. Only four years later, in *At Heaven's Gate*, the sense of tragedy will have turned somewhat sour and rancid to the taste, and Macbeth will have been replaced by smaller, meaner men.

At Heaven's Gate (1943)

The moral vacuum in modern society is depressingly evident in Warren's second novel, *At Heaven's Gate*—an ironic title, considering the poor damned souls therein. In fact, Warren has admitted that the novel was inspired by the seventh circle of Dante's *Inferno*, which holds those who are violators of nature. The novel is relatively weak in plot but exceptionally strong as a set of well-developed characterizations and an intricate web of personal relationships.

Jerry Calhoun is an intelligent, ambitious young man, who, as a college football hero, meets Bogan Murdock, the local business tycoon. Although Jerry graduates as a geologist, he blithely repudiates that career when Murdock offers him a job in his bank. Jerry sees in Murdock all the competence, self-assurance, and success that his own clumsy, dirt farmer father lacks. Jerry becomes Murdock's satellite and romances his beautiful daughter Sue.

Sue Murdock is a very confused young lady, raised in

luxury but contemptuous of the tyranny that her father
exercises over his family and associates. Her rebellion
leads her to cultivate unfashionable friends, local actors
and actresses, and seedy intellectuals, particularly the
cynical poet, Slim Sarrett. Sue tries to draw Jerry,
whom she has seduced, into this eccentric group, but he
despises them as much as her father does. Though Sue
and Jerry are engaged, she eventually walks out on him
when she realizes that he is content to be her father's
stooge.

Sue becomes Slim Sarrett's mistress, drawn by his
talent for glib analysis, his "colorful" family background as offspring of a barge captain and a whore (a
lineage Slim makes up for her special benefit), and his
apparent disregard for money, status, and all such
values dear to her father. Sue's eyes are opened about
Slim when one of his old friends shows up at the party,
inadvertently reveals Slim's ordinary middle-class origins, and indulges in a homosexual embrace with Slim
in the kitchen. Sue flees the party with Jason Sweetwater, a Marxist and professional labor organizer, and
soon becomes his mistress. Months later, after Sue has
had an abortion because Sweetwater does not believe in
marriage, Slim enters her apartment and strangles her.

Meanwhile, the financial empire and reputation of
Bogan Murdock crumbles when fraudulent land deals
put many of his subordinates in jail, including "Private" Porsum, once a World War I hero[2] and now
president of Murdock's bank, and Jerry, his vice-presi-
dent. Neither of them has been entirely conscious of
what has been going on behind the scenes, although
hardly innocent either in a situation in which they have
been Murdock's willing pawns. Also in jail is Murdock's Negro retainer, who is accused of Sue's murder.
Apparently, everyone will suffer more from these disasters than the paramount villains of the piece, Bogan
Murdock and Slim Sarrett.

Another occupant of the jail is a distant cousin of Private Porsum, Ashby Wyndham, an itinerant evangelist. He is there because one of his followers, a woman whom he had rescued from "the house of abominations," has shot a policeman. Wyndham's story is a subplot within the larger tale, a sad and touching account narrated in Wyndham's hill dialect—the story of his evil violence against his own brother, his subsequent conversion, and his life as a wanderer and preacher searching for absolution. It is an engrossing character study in its own right, exploring yet another kind of human failure to achieve a dream. Ashby's simplistic message of faith obviously does not prevent evil, even among his own converts, but his aspiration has a certain dignity when presented in conjunction with the guile and greed of Murdock and the amoral nihilism of Slim Sarrett. Moreover, the example of his rectitude is indirectly influential in destroying Murdock because it contributes to Private Porsum's decision to expose Murdock (and himself) publicly.

Thus Warren presents us with a modern inferno indeed, showing three levels of society, none of which offers a really viable system of values. One has a dismaying set of alternatives: the infamous alliance of politics and industry, the bohemian irresponsibility of the marginal artistic community, the one-answer idealism of the ardent Marxist, the ignorant religiosity of the back country, or a return to the farm to eke out a precarious living at the mercy of nature and unscrupulous politicians.

There are only two really humane persons, and they are somehow weak and ineffectual. One is a friend of Jerry's, Duckfoot Blake, who is a part of Murdock's organization but has enough independence and moral sense to resign when he perceives fraud in company transactions. Duckfoot is a rather sad, emotionally crippled person, who has made some compromises and accommodations to the grimy world of business. Perhaps his usually painful feet are vaguely symbolic of his discomfort with the road he has chosen.

The other decent person is Jerry's father, an inept but gentle human being, who with infinite patience feeds and cares for a paralyzed old aunt and puts up with a vicious-tongued, crippled brother. This household is hardly paradise, but it is a place where the father cares for the human beings to whom he owes family allegiance, no matter what their weaknesses. In this virtue, he is akin to Warren's father, who learned to take joy in his family obligations.

It is this large capacity for forgiveness and acceptance, however, that Jerry hates most about his father, for it reveals to Jerry at last the real nature of his own ruthlessness. As he lies down again in his childhood bed, he knows that not only has he despised his aunt and uncle, but has wished his father dead. This is the bottom line of Jerry's earned self-knowledge. And he has learned, of course, that Murdock, the surrogate father he has admired and emulated, is "hollow to the core," as Conrad would put it.

Slim Sarrett is one of the most subtle creations in this novel, the most purely satanic and ironically the closest to Warren himself. If ever a writer has projected imaginatively his own dark shadow, it is Warren in this characterization. Perhaps he did not intend it that way. As a matter of fact, he has said "that character was almost a portrait of a person I knew, the closest portrait I've ever done in a piece of fiction."[3] If Sarrett was not a Mr. Hyde that Warren imagined in himself, then I suspect the real model exemplified what Warren most feared to become —the intellectual without heart.

One of the characteristics attributed to Satan is that he wants to be his own father, that is, he wants to be self-created, without obligation to anyone, like Lucifer trying to displace God the Father. Slim Sarrett obliterates his real father by creating a purely imaginary one, then disposing of him by saying that he died in a barge explosion. He further diffuses even that father-image by deciding that, since his mother was a prostitute, his father was not one man but many, using the physical paternity as a metaphor for the supposed autonomy of the poet. "For the artist has no father. Only a multiplicity of fathers, who don't owe him a thing. Not a damned thing. . . . And therefore, the artist is free, because he doesn't owe them anything either."

Though Slim Sarrett has created a false identity, he can also bend the truth to his own uses. What really wins over Sue Murdock to consider Slim a source of strength and rectitude is his precise analysis of her father, delivered calmly to his face: "You represent to me the special disease of our time, the abstract passion for power, a vanity springing from an awareness of the emptiness and unreality of the self which can only attempt to become real and human by the oppression of people who manage to retain some shreds of reality and humanity." In this sentiment Slim surely speaks for Warren himself, with all his distrust of industrial-political alliances. Leonard Casper, in *Robert Penn Warren: The Dark and Bloody Ground*, says that "Warren borrowed from the actual careers of such men as Luke Lea of Tennessee, one-time United States senator and convicted bank manipulator, imprisoned for the multimillion-dollar failure of the Asheville Central Bank and Trust Company."[4]

Sarrett speaks for Warren elsewhere in the novel, too, expressing the author's view of tragedy ("The tragic flaw in the Shakespearean hero is a defect in self-knowledge") and Warren's idea of impurity in poetry:

"The successful man—saint, politician, pickpocket, scholar, sensualist, costermonger—offers only the smooth surface, like an egg. Insofar as he is truly successful, he has no story. He is pure. But poetry is concerned only with failure, distortion, imbalance —with impurity. And poetry itself is impurity. The pure cry of

pain is not poetry. The pure gasp and sign of love is not poetry.
Poetry is the impurity which an active being secretes to become
pure. It is the glitter of pus, richer than Ind, the monument of
dung, the oyster's pearl."

Warren expressed these sentiments in one of his best-
known essays on critical principles, "Pure and Impure
Poetry," first published in *Sewanee Review* and the same year
as *At Heaven's Gate* and later included in his *Collected Essays*.

It is curious that a character so close to having the
convictions of his author (and incidentally rather like him
in appearance, perhaps) should be so convincingly evil.
Because of his cold-bloodedness, Sarrett is less attractive
than the religious Dostoevsky's renowned atheist, Ivan
Karamazov, who said "If God does not exist, then all
things are possible." Yet these two are similar in that they
destroy all limits on human behavior and thus leave man
exposed to the potential hideousness of his own unbridled
impulses.

In Slim Sarrett, Warren has imposed his distinctive
signature, in Leslie Fiedler's terms, upon the Satan
archetype. Warren would never be tempted, as Jerry is, by
Bogan Murdock. It is Slim's satanic sin of intellectual
pride that can tempt an intellectual, particularly if he is
also something of a heretic. But Warren makes very clear
that Slim is as vain and manipulative in his own way
as Murdock, and less disciplined. Warren has shown that
intellect alone cannot protect its possessor from feelings of
humiliation and impulses to violence. Both Sarrett's and
Jerry's hidden desire to kill their fathers may reflect, in
some distorted way of course, Warren's old feeling of guilt
for having stolen his father's life by becoming a poet.

Early Poetry

Warren's poetry during these early years of his career also
centers on themes of passage from the prelapsarian world

into a polluted present, in which the soul feels alienated and alone and in desperate need of purification. Warren develops a repertoire of imagery for the myth of the fall, for the sense of guilt and deprivation that accompanies action in the world of time, for various ways to recapture or remember the timelessness of the prelapsarian world. The desire to blend back into the anonymity of nature is expressed often in water imagery, as in "Bearded Oaks," where the persona and his companion lying in the grass seem to be immersed in the ocean. "The oaks, how subtle and marine/Bearded, and all the layered light/Above them swims; . . ." This experience is recognized as the state of timelessness to which the living return.

> We live in time so little time
> And we learn all so painfully,
> That we may spare this hour's term
> To practice for eternity.[5]

Warren often uses birds to indicate the flight of the soul—again, an archetypal symbol of very ancient origin but very close to Warren's actual experience. His most striking use of the hawk as symbol of the soul is a recent one, "Red-Tail Hawk and Pyre of Youth" in *Now and Then: Poems 1976–1978*. This is probably the only poem in existence that dwells upon the technique of taxidermy, one of those obscure skills Warren mastered as a youth. The literary predecessor of the hawk that Warren shot and stuffed as a boy is the hawk in his early "Picnic Remembered":

> The *then*, the *now*: each cenotaph
> Of the other, and proclaims it dead.
> Or is the soul a hawk that, fled
> On glimmering wings past vision's path,
> Reflects the last gleam to us here
> Though sun is sunk and darkness near
> —Uncharted Truth's high heliograph?

"Love's Parable," a poem as metaphysical as any by John Donne, traces the downfall of an ideal love. It begins with an elaborate conceit that likens the attraction of the lovers to that between a war-torn populace and a foreign prince who seems to offer a "new felicity": "Once, each to each, such aliens, we." Both the bliss of early love and its utter heedlessness of the future emerge in curious images of careless destructiveness:

> Then miracle was corner-cheap;
> And we, like ignorant quarriers,
> Ransacked the careless earth to heap
> For highways our most precious ores;
> Or like the blockhead masons who
> Burnt Rome's best grandeur for its lime,
> And for their slattern hovels threw
> Down monuments of a nobler time.

Eventually love itself deteriorates to some shared ritual of lust, and the persona wonders, "Are we but mirror to the world?/Or does the world our ruin reflect . . . ?" Thus, the disorder of society and the disorder of personal relationships reflect and reinforce each other.

Probably the best known and most striking of Warren's poems in his early period is "The Ballad of Billie Potts," another version of the archetypal fall and eventual return to the place of origin. Here, the Oedipal pattern suggested in *At Heaven's Gate*, in which the fallen son desires to kill the father, is curiously reversed. Billie Potts, the father, who has preceded his son out of God's grace, murders his son. The poem is based on a frontier legend about a man who kept an inn to serve early travelers going West, but he shared in the booty of bandits for providing them with advance information about the routes of these travelers, so that they could be ambushed and robbed.

Billy Potts and his wife have a big, hulking son, whom they both adore. The son, thinking he will prove his value to his father, attempts to kill and rob a stranger by himself instead of conveying the information to more experienced killers. He botches the job and returns home in humiliation. His father, in anger, turns him out to make his fortune as best he can. Many years later, the son, having prospered out West, returns in triumph, sporting a heavy beard, a handsome coat, and a bag of gold. He conceals his identity for a while, hoping to tease his parents, but they, thinking he is just another traveler, murder him for his money. The parents learn too late, through an identifying birthmark, that they have killed the only person they ever loved. This archetypal myth of violence between father and son has an especially ironic twist since not only is the son destroyed, but also the father, in emotional terms, because of his fatal "flaw" of love in an otherwise evil nature.

Warren captures the rhyming, lilting, but occasionally uneven rhythm of folk ballad, its colloquial language combined with an occasionally oracular tone. Here is the third stanza:

> They had a big boy with fuzz on his chin
> So tall he ducked the door when he came in,
> A clabber-headed bastard with snot in his nose
> And big red wrists hanging out of his clothes
> And a whicker when he laughed where his father had a
>   bellow
> In the section between the rivers.
> They called him Little Billie.
> He was their darling.

The land "between the rivers," which is a repeated refrain (one of the characteristics of ballad), refers to a section between the Cumberland and the Tennessee rivers. Victor Strandberg, who has written extensively about Warren's poetry, suggests that the setting has overtones of the beginning of civilization between the Tigris and the Euphrates rivers, where many supposed that the Garden of Eden was situated.[6]

The comment upon the action, which universalizes the legend, appears in parentheses. Warren uses the

second person here, as he does in a number of poems, to
indicate the conscious self, which does not recognize the
unconscious, the shadow-self. What at first seems a
simple device to show "you" what it was like in those
days—a guided tour of the past, so to speak—becomes a
way of involving the hypothetical reader, as conscious
ego, in a somber psychodrama. Strandberg has explained this process convincingly and praises "The
Ballad of Billie Potts" as the poem that most successfully
combines Warren's typical themes. "In 'The Ballad of
Billie Potts,' Warren's three ground themes of passage,
the undiscovered self, and mysticism fuse for the first
time into his single paramount theme of identity."[7]

The theme of passage is essentially a variation of the
fall of man, whereby each person, by an act of will,
passes from the innocence of childhood, the prelapsarian
world, into the fallen world of the fathers (here dramatized as Little Billie's willful participation in his father's
crimes). This theme is not only typical of Warren's work
but also typically American, since part of the popular
conception of the American wilderness was as an
untouched Eden, where one could start life afresh like a
new Adam or like Huckleberry Finn on the bosom of the
great river.

According to psychoanalytic theory, with the fall
(that is, the conscious choice of evil) the personality
begins to split. What is perceived as evil in oneself is
usually repressed into the subconscious, to become what
Jung called the shadow (expressed in Gothic literature as
the doppelgänger). In order to attain self-knowledge, the
conscious self (the "you" of the poem) must acknowledge
this alter ego (here dramatized as the evil father to whom
the young man returns). That his message, quite aside
from the gruesome story, is intended for a wider
application becomes clear when the commentary switch-
es from Little Billie's experience to the hypothetical
reader's:

> Though your luck held and the market was always
>   satisfactory
> Though the letter always came and your lovers were
>   always true,
> Though you always received the respect due to your
>   position,
> Though your hand never failed of its cunning and your
>   glands always thoroughly knew their business,
> Though your conscience was easy and you were assured
>   of your innocence,
> You became gradually aware that something was missing
>   from the picture,
> And upon closer inspection exclaimed: "Why, I'm not
>   in it at all!"
> Which was perfectly true.

The real "I" is "not in it at all" because these lines refer only to the conscious ego and its supposed triumphs in surface reality. The true "I," one's real identity, must acknowledge the participation of the shadow in the unified self, which includes good and evil, triumph and defeat.

The mysticism that Strandberg notes as one of the themes in Warren's poetry refers especially to the pantheistic element that emerges at the end of "Billie Potts" and elsewhere. The final meditation is almost a benediction, likening the wanderer's return (not just Little Billie's now, but your own also) to the mysterious natural forces that direct the salmon's return to the "high pool" of his birth, with its ambiguous implications of both innocence and death.

> The salmon heaves at the fall, and, wanderer, you
> Heave at the great fall of Time, and gorgeous, gleam
> In the powerful arc, and anger and outrage like dew,
> In your plunge, fling, and plunge to the thunderous
>   stream:
> Back to the silence, back to the pool, back
> To the high pool, motionless, and the unmurmuring
>   dream.

And you, wanderer. Back.
Brother to pinion and the pious fin that cleave
Their innocence of air and the disinfectant flood
And wing and welter and weave
The long compulsion and the circuit hope
Back,
And bear through that limitless and devouring fluidity
The itch and humble promise which is home.
And the father waits for the son.

One of the philosophic constants in Warren's poetry is that past, present, and future may seem to interpenetrate, so that all time exists simultaneously and, perhaps, everlastingly—which seems to be as close as Warren ever comes to a belief in immortality.

Another famous poem of the period 1923 to 1943 is "Original Sin: A Short Story." It is often quoted by critics, because sooner or later everyone must deal with the idea of original sin, which Warren has salvaged from conventional Christianity. Original sin is not, however, something inherited, but rather something committed by each person, like Little Billie's assault on the stranger. All are fallen, though the precise circumstance of the fall may grow dim in memory. This particular poem suggests something foolish and archaic about original sin, which follows you (the conscious ego) through life like some disreputable ghost—more of a nuisance than anything else, perhaps, because one doesn't know what to do with it. It is one of Warren's gentler and more humorous treatments of this mournful topic, full of arresting images. Warren has said of this poem, "The story is about the personal past and the past behind the personal past, I suppose, and the problem that contemplating this past makes for us in our world of mobility and disorientation."[8]

Nodding, its great head rattling like a gourd,
And locks like seaweed strung on the stinking stone,
The nightmare stumbles past, and you have heard

It fumble your door before it whimpers and is gone:
It acts like the old hound that used to snuffle your door and
　　moan.

You thought you had lost it when you left Omaha,
For it seemed connected then with your grandpa, who
Had a wen on his forehead and sat on the veranda
To finger the precious protuberance, as was his habit to do,
Which glinted in sun like rough garnet or the rich old brain
　　bulging through.

Here, as in "Billie Potts," the sin is made visible by the old person, though he is not intended to be an especially evil character. Indeed, he may be more like the aged Oedipus, knowing and acknowledging his flaw and carrying it openly, or Hester Prynne wearing her scarlet letter. He is, nevertheless, testimony of the fallen world.

A most cogent discussion of this poem is in an address by Cleanth Brooks called "Poetry in the Age of Anxiety."[9] Brooks treats the poem as a critique of rationality; the monster represents the ineradicable, nonrational elements of man, which are an affront to our pride in reason. Thus, the nightmare may be compared with the imbecile but also with the old hound, the old horse, and even the old mother, who loves irrationally. In spite of the idiotic and dangerous possibilities of the nonrational, such human virtues as loyalty, sympathy, and love are equally subrational.

After *Selected Poems 1923–1943*, Warren found it impossible to complete short poems for almost ten years. The final years of his unhappy first marriage, which may or may not be reflected in the somber "Love's Parable," were devoted to a perfecting of fictional techniques. In *All the King's Men*, Warren was to examine again the fall from innocence, the tragedy of fathers and sons, and the necessity for self-knowledge. His perception of the Bogan Murdocks of this world had deepened, however, suggesting that such persons exist because they fulfill some unrecognized need in the populace whose confidence they exploit.

3

The Dream Sea of Ideas:
Prose Period, 1944–1950

A man that is born falls into a dream like a man who falls into the sea.

—Joseph Conrad

During the decade of the forties, Warren wrote his best fiction and some excellent criticism. He produced *All the King's Men*, a number of short stories, and the novel based loosely on the life of Jeroboam Beauchamp, *World Enough and Time*. Brooks and Warren continued to produce textbooks: their *Modern Rhetoric*, first published in 1949, was issued in 1950 and thereafter as *Fundamentals of Good Writing: A Handbook of Modern Rhetoric*. The discussion of Warren's criticism will be confined here to those works contained in *Selected Essays* (1958). They extend actually from the note on Thomas Wolfe in 1935 through the essay on Katherine Anne Porter in 1952, but most fall within the decade of the forties.

Criticism

We have already noted that in 1942 Warren was ironically putting into the mouth of Slim Sarrett his important concept of impurity in poetry. In his essay on "Pure and Impure Poetry" in *Selected Essays* he says, "Poetry wants to be pure, but poems do not." Therefore, they may occasionally "mar themselves with cacophonies, jagged rhythms, ugly words and ugly thoughts, colloquialisms, clichés, sterile technical terms, headwork and argument, self-contradictions, clevernesses, irony, realism—all things which call us back to the world of prose and imperfection." The presumed purity of poetry requires working through the ambiguities and ironies which impede such purity.

In other words, a poem, to be good, must earn itself. It is a motion toward a point of rest, but if it is not a resisted motion, it is motion of no consequence. For example, a poem which depends upon stock materials and stock responses is simply a toboggan slide, or a fall through space. And the good poem must, in some way, involve the resistances; it must carry something of the context of its own creation; it must come to terms with Mercutio.

The reference to Mercutio points to his excellent illustration of the principle of impurity in *Romeo and Juliet*. The famous garden scene between the young lovers would seem to be an example of purity in poems, the expression of love as yet unsullied by exploitation or carnality. But its special poignancy depends upon our realization that on the other side of the garden wall Mercutio is making bawdy jokes. Moreover, the earthy nurse, standing in the wings, and even Juliet herself ("Swear not by the inconstant moon . . .") temper the lofty romanticism of Romeo. The effect is not to destroy the principle of perfect romantic love but to show how very fragile, and therefore precious, such experience is.

Warren's essay on Hemingway is excellent, particularly for showing Hemingway's relationship to the contemporary themes of alienation and rebellion and what Warren calls the cult of sensation, which occasionally becomes, as in *A Farewell to Arms*, the cult of true love, expressed in sensual terms. Warren compares Hemingway's romantic anti-intellectualism with the outlooks of such writers as Wordsworth, Tennyson, and Hardy. Hemingway is most successful, Warren says, when he accepts the limitations of his own premises. Warren therefore prefers *A Farewell to Arms* to the later, more ambitious novel *For Whom the Bell Tolls*.

In "The Themes of Robert Frost," Warren examines the symbol of the dark woods in several of Frost's poems. Warren often uses the woods symbolically himself in poetry; whether he was influenced by Frost in this or simply found a similar affinity for woods and their literary suggestiveness is hard to say. He also examines "After Apple-Picking," one of the very best of Frost's lyrics.

Warren's critical attention tends to gravitate to those writers whose views he shares. I have noted this earlier in his listing of the thematic concerns of Nathaniel Hawthorne, so like his own. In *Selected Essays*, the most obvious parallel to his own attitudes is found in the essay on William Faulkner, but parts of his essays on Conrad and Coleridge are also self-revelatory. Warren and Faulkner share, of course, the concerns of the Southern Agrarians regarding the exploitation of nature and the substitution of commercial success for older notions of virtue, truth, and endurance. Thus, the following paragraph, though immediately qualified by the observation that "there never was a golden age in which man was simple and complete," is as pertinent to *At Heaven's Gate* as it is to Faulkner's work:

The Faulkner legend is not merely a legend of the South but of a general plight and problem. The modern world is in moral confusion. It does suffer from a lack of discipline, of sanction, of community of values, of a sense of mission. We don't have to go to Faulkner to find that out—or to find that it is a world in which self-interest, workableness, success provide the standards of conduct. It was a Yankee who first referred to the bitch goddess Success. It is a world in which the individual has lost his relation to society, the world of the power state in which man is a cipher. It is a world in which man is the victim of abstraction and mechanism, or at least, at moments, feels himself to be. It can look back nostalgically upon various worlds of the past, Dante's world of the Catholic synthesis, Shakespeare's world of Renaissance energy, or the world of our grandfathers who lived before Shiloh and Gettysburg, and feel loss of traditional values and despair in its own aimlessness and fragmentation . . . a world in which men were . . . more simple and complete.

Warren defends Faulkner effectively against complaints of racism and snobbery. He also describes Faulkner's view of human nature with one of his own favorite terms, *original sin*, which he equates here with "the sin of use, exploitation, violation" of nature or of other human beings. Thus, slavery is one of the many forms of that original sin, which the South must redeem.

Warren deals lovingly with the works of one of his long-time friends in "Irony With a Center: Katherine Anne Porter." Warren says that "Many of her stories are unsurpassed in modern fiction . . ." His perceptive discussion of "Flowering Judas," "Noon Wine," and "Old Mortality" demonstrates both the nature and method of Porter's irony. "Old Mortality" is especially intriguing to Warren because of its subtle examination of the making of family legends.

Warren's essay on " 'The Great Mirage': Conrad and *Nostromo*" is surely one of the most cogent in Conrad criticism. Conrad and Warren are kindred spirits; though not at all false to Conrad, Warren's interpretation can often seem a meditation on his own attitudes toward man and nature. Warren's explication of the enigmatic speech of Stein at the heart of *Lord Jim* is probably as good as or better than any other offered by critics, and it says something about Warren's use of dream and water imagery as well. The symbolic passage from Conrad goes like this:

A man that is born falls into a dream like a man who falls into the sea. If he tries to climb out into the air as inexperienced people endeavor to do, he drowns—*nicht wahr*? . . . No! I tell you! The way is to the destructive element submit yourself, and with the exertions of your hands and feet in the water make the deep, deep sea keep you up.

Warren interprets the dream here as "man's necessity to justify himself by the 'idea,' to idealize himself and his actions into moral significance of some order, to find sanctions." The destructiveness of the dream arises from man's nature as an egotistical animal with savage impulses, not completely adapted to the dream sea of ideas. Warren goes on to explain:

> Those men who take the purely "natural" view, who try to climb out of the sea, who deny the dream and man's necessity to submit to the idea, who refuse to create values that are, quite literally, "supernatural" and therefore human, are destroyed by the dream. They drown in it, and their agony is the agony of their frustrated humanity.

The one who learns to swim instead of drowning in the unnatural sea of ideas is the one who realizes that the values he creates are illusion, but that "the illusion is necessary, is infinitely precious, is the mark of his human achievement, and is, in the end, his only truth."

Warren classifies thematic elements in Conrad's stories as built around: (1) the man who lacks imagination but clings to fidelity and duty (like the old captain in *Youth*), (2) the sinner against human solidarity and the human mission (like Kurtz in *Heart of Darkness* and Decoud in *Nostromo*), (3) the redeemed sinner (Lord Jim, Dr. Monygham in *Nostromo*). Conrad is most interested in the last—"And the crisis of this story comes when the hero recognizes the terms on which he may be saved, the moment, to take Morton Zabel's phrase, of the 'terror of the awakening.'"

One might note that in Warren's novel *At Heaven's Gate*, Jerry's father fits the pattern of natural rectitude (1. above) and Slim Sarrett is certainly the sinner described in 2. No one seems to be redeemed there, although Jerry might have a chance in a hypothetical future. Redemption does enter into other novels of this period, however, since Burden in *All the King's Men* and perhaps even the murderer in *World Enough and Time* achieve some kind of absolution. Warren and Conrad share this deep obsession with the need for redemption, and although the sentiment is religious and may, on occasion, use Christian imagery, it is consistently humanistic in emphasis. The world they both recognize is a naturalistic one, but man must live in two worlds, the world of fact and the world of idea, which he creates himself. This submission to the idea is analogous to Hemingway's "code" of the hunter, the fisherman, the bullfighter, or the soldier, which provides existential meaning in a meaningless world. Hemingway's treatment of this theme is like a solitary instrument or lonely voice singing in the mountains; Conrad's or Warren's is like an orchestra, more complex, compounded by deep resonances, more foreboding at times, but perhaps less clear and "pure" in effect.

Warren discusses certain contradictions or seeming inconsistencies which may be found in Conrad's nonfiction utterances—and Warren may share these contradictions, too. Conrad once wrote to Galsworthy, "Scepticism, the tonic of minds, the tonic of life, the agent of truth—the way of art and salvation" (This sounds like Decoud or Slim Sarrett.) Yet, at other times, he wrote of the "solidarity of all mankind in simple ideas and emotions" and that "For the great mass of mankind the only saving grace that is needed is steady fidelity to what is nearest to hand and heart in the short moment of each human effort"—sentiments that seem to belie his own tortured inwardness and skepticism.

I suspect that these careful investigations of Conrad's art have had a diffuse, but powerful influence on the ideas and imagery of many of Warren's works—*Meet Me in the Green Glen*, for instance, with its variation of the "natural man," reminiscent of *Nostromo*. Warren calls the novel *Nostromo* "a study in the definition and necessity of illusion," an issue that Warren also addresses in such novels as *Wilderness* and *World Enough and Time*. To delineate influences on Warren's work, however, is always a guessing game, for Warren is never guilty of slavish imitation; he digests his reading of other writers' works so thoroughly that they become part of his personal store of ideas and images.

The longest and most complex study in *Selected Essays*, "A Poem of Pure Imagination: An Experiment in Reading," deals with Coleridge's "The Rime of the Ancient Mariner," which may be suspected to have had some obscure impact on Warren's *Brother to Dragons*. There is some similarity of theme in spite of the radical difference in degree of realism, since the murderer of the slave in Warren's poem is, in one ironic sense, Jefferson's albatross, and certainly slavery is the South's albatross. Moreover, the sheer audacity of the form of the composition may be due, in part, to Coleridge's example, the character RPW taking the place of the explanatory gloss in "The Ancient Mariner."

Warren's essay includes a detailed consideration of most of the critical controversies that have surrounded "The Ancient Mariner." He declares absurd the efforts of some critics to reduce the poem to an allegory by equating the pilot with the church, the pilot's boy with the clergy, the hermit with "enlightened religion." There is a cogent discussion on the complexity and psychological functioning of symbolism and its superiority, in imaginative terms, to allegory.

Warren deals at some length with the objection, sometimes expressed, that the mariner's crime is unmotivated or that it is simply frivolous—all that fuss about killing a bird? In fact, its very lack of motivation is one of the factors that establishes the killing as an especially perverse act, allied to original sin. The albatross is called "the pious bird of good omen" and hailed in God's name "as if it had been a Christian soul, . . ." The killing is a crime against nature and therefore a crime against God. Warren cites Edgar Allan Poe's use of the same kind of

analogy between wanton creature killing and mortal sin
in "The Black Cat," in which the protagonist perversely
hangs his affectionate cat. Both cases of unmotivated
killing are symbolic of a satanic element in the will.

Warren explains the killing of the albatross as a
crime against the imagination also. He suggests that the
poem has a primary theme, which is the sacramental
vision, or the theme of the "one life," culminating in the
message explicitly stated in the fable ("He prayeth best,
who loveth best/All things both great and small; . . .")
But it has a secondary theme (not, however, less important) concerning the imagination.

Warren explains Coleridge's poem in the light of a
general effort, common to other Romantic poets (Keats,
Shelley, Wordsworth) as well, to combine moral and
aesthetic concerns as aspects of the same activity, the
creative activity. Truth is beauty, beauty truth, as Keats
put it, and morality is part of the same mental function.
"Now," says Warren, "my argument is that 'The
Ancient Mariner' is, first, written *out* of this general
belief, and second, written *about* this general belief."

Warren's essay can be helpful to all students of
Romantic literature and Romantic aesthetic theory. It
has, as well, a more general relevance to modern
thought, since the struggle of the Romantics to justify
"nonscientific" functions of the mind has hardly been
won. The poet, the artist, may feel even more threatened
now than in the past century. The impulse to examine
closely one of the most fantastic creations of the Romantic poets issues partly, no doubt, from objective scholarly
curiosity, but it may also reflect a more personal compulsion in Warren, a need to establish for himself the
function and justification of poetic creativity. Warren has
always spoken of the writing of poems as a process of
self-discovery, and I believe that much of his literary
criticism serves a similar function. Perhaps it does for all
truly committed critics.

Short Stories

Warren's book of short stories, *Circus in the Attic* (1947), contains stories actually written between 1930 and 1946, including "Prime Leaf," which preceded his novel *Night Rider*. "Prime Leaf" focuses on the relationships between three generations of one family. The elder Mr. Hardin is quite similar to the elder Todd in *Night Rider*: he follows a personal code of honor, withdrawing from the tobacco growers' association when night riders start burning uncooperative farmers' barns. His son wants to stay in but out of loyalty to his father also withdraws. This choice of allegiance results in the son's assassination and the burning of their tobacco barn. The child is left with the burden of grief and bitterness, the honorable grandfather presumably with an added element of guilt.

"The Circus in the Attic," title story of the volume, is a rather melancholy tale of human lives immersed in varying degrees of self-deception and isolation. It traces the undistinguished life of a delicate, obedient, small-town boy, Bolton Lovehart, who runs off with a circus when he is sixteen. He is apprehended, however, and brought back home. The boy remains there, dominated by his somewhat neurotic mother, long after his father's death. His mother becomes an invalid and is apparently quite happy as the sole object of her son's affection. Bolton's only secret defiance is to retire in the evenings to the attic, where he is presumably writing a book. Actually, most of his time is spent carving and painting toy circus figures, at which he becomes quite skilled.

Eventually, his mother dies and he loses interest in his circus in the attic. He marries a widow and acquires a stepson, of whom he is fond. After the stepson is killed in World War II, Bolton finds a use for his circus in the attic. He donates his carvings to be sold at a bazaar to raise money for the Red Cross. He feels that he has vindicated or expiated his old defiance of his mother and made some gesture for his stepson.

The family relationships are neither as clear nor quite as convincing as those in "Prime Leaf." Perhaps the best theme for the story is its assertion at one point that ". . . people always believe what truth they have to believe to go on being the way they are." "The way they are" seems strangely empty where nothing really matters for very long. Gross errors in social roles can be born with equanimity, even with pleasure, through the mind's capacity to compensate for or exploit the accidents of fate.

Thus, the story is also, like "The Ancient Mariner," an exploration of the function of imaginative creativity, especially its quality of compensating for the restrictions of a drab reality. The attic is apparently a metaphor for the human mind, where our subjective stories are created, our private myths developed. This private myth is here shown in conjunction with the public myth of history with its stories of wartime valor, in both the past and the present. The local monuments to Civil War heroes celebrate undistinguished men, more frightened than heroic, and Bolton's stepson is actually a vain and shallow youth. Although during the war the soldiers stationed in the area are potential heroes and, therefore, honored guests, after the war the soldiers become nuisances to the community. Lovehart is the only one who continues to view them as worthy of special respect.

One of the most successful stories is "The Patented Gate and the Mean Hamburger." Warren describes the poor dirt farmer Jeff York with the utmost precision. "The big hands, with the knotted, cracked joints and the square, horn-thick nails, hang loose off the wristbone like clumsy, homemade tools hung on the wall of a shed after work." York looks like a thousand other men of his class, but he is significantly different. The others are sharecroppers, but he, by many years of unremitting toil, has acquired not only his own place but also a patented gate, which can be

opened and closed without getting down from a wagon or
buggy. The gate is his proudest possession, the badge of
his determination and well-earned success.

York has a nondescript little wife, much younger
than he, and three towheaded youngsters. The highlight
of their uneventful lives is the Saturday ritual of going to
town for supplies and getting hamburgers at the Dew
Drop Inn Diner. When the proprietor of the restaurant
decides to sell out and move elsewhere, the townspeople
are amazed that the seemingly subservient Mrs. York
somehow persuades her hard-bitten husband to sell his
farm so they can buy the diner. The former owner teaches
her how to sling a "mean hamburger," and York stoically
repairs and paints the establishment. Then he walks off
into the country and hangs himself on the patented gate he
had once owned. The shy, little widow, though grief-
stricken, soon becomes an outgoing and popular proprietor of the town's most successful eating place. It is an
added irony, of course, that the patented gate, symbolic to
York of his success as a farmer, is also a symbol of the
modern technology and the urban values that destroy
him.

Some of the stories in the volume are entwined with
people and events that Warren knew as a child. "When
the Light Gets Green," for instance, was undoubtedly
inspired by Warren's grandfather Penn. The story has
little plot but suggests the way a child perceives old age
and comes to realize the relative helplessness of human
beings in the face of nature. "Goodwood Comes Back" is a
characterization based on a childhood friend of Warren's
who became a baseball pitcher in the big league but
dropped out because of alcoholism and returned to a rural
Kentucky farm. It is an examination, partly, of the
difference in life-style between most urban people and the
backwoodsman who loves hunting and hunting dogs.
Warren has combined his friend's basic story with other
elements from real life, occasions of unexpected violence

among isolated families. Goodwood is shot by his
brother-in-law.

Warren's style in these stories is naturalistic, the
point of view usually objective. A close look at the region,
the people, the social-economic situation is balanced by
an ironic distance from the emotional turmoil that
presumably boils under the surface. We do not see farmer
York being persuaded to give up what he has struggled for
all his life. There is some general discussion in "Goodwood Comes Back" of what happens when people live in
extreme isolation from society, but we do not know why
Goodwood was shot by his brother-in-law. Sometimes
objectivity blends into sardonic black humor, as in "The
Confession of Brother Grimes." Brother Grimes has
always made much of God's justice and always preached
that God administers punishments that fit the crimes.
After a series of disasters, including the accidental death
of his wife when she rides with a drunken driver, Brother
Grimes searches his heart and confesses to his congrega-
tion (in support of his thesis about God's justice) that he
has lived a lie and is therefore responsible for these
tragedies: he has been dyeing his hair for the last twenty
years!

The best known and most often anthologized of the
stories is "Blackberry Winter," which has many autobiographical elements. Like so much of Warren's poetry
involving childhood experience, it captures the way in
which children become aware of the suffering and
disillusionment associated with adult life. It is a story of
the passage from the naïve paradise of expectation into the
blemished reality of adults. This theme is subtly suggested
from the very first, when the nine-year-old boy is in a
contest of wills with his mother about whether he should
go outside barefoot. The fact that it is June is sufficient
reason, in the boy's mind, for going barefoot, in spite of the
obvious reality of an unseasonable cold spell.

The very real chill of an inhospitable world after a

"gully-washer" is but one detail of a series of impressions the child accumulates that day: the sinister urban tramp who earns fifty cents by gathering up and burning the drowned chicks strewn in the mud of the chicken yard; the dead cow that bobs in the flooding river; the suggestive question of a sharecropper's young son, "Reckon anybody ever et drownt cow?" and the old soldier's rejoinder ". . . a man will eat anything when the time comes"; the junk that washes out from under the cabin of Dellie and Jeff, the "white folks' niggers" who refuse to be shiftless and careless and dirty like so many of the other Negro tenants and whose pride results in constant badgering of little Jebb by other Negro children; the mysterious sickness of Delli, which old Jeff calls "woman-misery . . . Hit just comes on 'em when the time come . . . Hit is the change of life and time."

These hints of something that happens in time that the boy does not understand induce him to follow the miserable tramp, with his incongruous city clothes, with questions: "Where did you come from? . . . Where are you going?" only to be met with the warning, "You don't stop following me and I cut yore throat, you little son-of-a-bitch." The narrator reveals now that these events occurred thirty-five years ago, and since then Father, Mother, and Delli are all dead and his chum, little Jebb, is in the penitentiary for killing another Negro. The narrator remembers the tramp's warning and knowing well the pain and frustration of the world closes with, "But I did follow him, all the years."

All the King's Men (1946)

To turn to Warren's justly acclaimed *All the King's Men* is to reconsider many of the themes already proposed in short stories, novels, and criticism. Here again we struggle with the sense of guilt and the need for expiation, the love-hate relationship between fathers and sons, the devastating alternatives of drowning in the dream sea of ideas or denying one's humanity on the arid land of fact, the necessity for balancing precariously between the abyss of nature and the abyss of self. As someone has said of Hamlet, this is a story of a man who does not know himself or, more accurately, of several men who do not know themselves: Willie Stark, who thinks he can use evil means to achieve good ends; Jack Burden, who tries to avoid guilt by running away or simply not seeing it, who does not recognize his own father and inadvertently kills him; Judge Irwin, representative of the old genteel tradition, who literally forgets his original sin; Adam Stanton, the puritan idealist, who drowns when he climbs out of the sea of ideas to kill Willie Stark.

The superiority of *All the King's Men* over former novels is partly a technical one, the mastery of point of view. The narrative voice of the cynical Jack Burden provides a unity and clarity lacking in *At Heaven's Gate*. That novel suffers from considerable uncertainty as to who the protagonist really is, Jerry or his one-time girlfriend, Sue Murdock, who dominates long passages at the heart of the novel, where Jerry is almost irrelevant. *All the King's Men* also has a double focus of interest in Willie Stark and Jack Burden, but the doubleness, instead of scattering interest, adds a peculiar depth. Both are continuously present because Willie is seen through Burden's eyes. Willie Stark is important for himself but more important as the most significant fact in Burden's existential dilemma.

Most readers are probably familiar with the plot. It concerns the rise to power of a man of the people, a man (like Huey Long) who fills some need for a folk hero who knows from experience the wretchedness of the poor and who will presumably succor the miserable and build roads and bridges and hospitals to serve the common man. Willie Stark is a cunning, hardworking, expedient politician.

Willie attains power partly by understanding and controlling other men, such as the unscrupulous Tiny Duffy, who is eminently suited to any political dirty work. The narrator, Jack Burden, is an ex-newspaperman and ex–graduate student in history, valuable partly for his research skills. Burden's task at the outset of the story is to "find something" on his father's old friend, Judge Irwin, who has always been like a father to Jack. Judge Irwin has come out for Willie's opponent in the upcoming election.

Jack pursues this investigation of Irwin with a curious dissociation of sensibility, convinced, on the one hand, that there can be no crime in what he calls the "Case of the Upright Judge," and on the other that Willie's assessment of human nature may, after all, be accurate. Willie's answer to Jack's assurance that there can be nothing dishonorable in Irwin's past is reiterated three times in the novel: "Man is conceived in sin and born in corruption and he passeth from the stink of the didie to the stench of the shroud. There is always something."

Jack Burden does, indeed, find something out of the forgotten past. Not only did the upright judge once accept a bribe, but he was protected by the equally immaculate Governor Stanton, father of Adam and Anne, Burden's dearest childhood friends. Burden holds this guilty knowledge until Anne herself asks him to convince Adam, now a celebrated surgeon, that he should accept the directorship of the medical center Willie wants to build. Jack understands that the only way to influence Adam in this respect is to change his mind about the nature of the world—to break his conviction that good and evil can be kept separate. How better to achieve this than to reveal that the idealized father and the irreproachable Judge Irwin were themselves guilty of political crimes?

The bitter knowledge of his father's expedient

compromise with honor has the desired effect on the puritanical Adam. He makes an uneasy alliance with Willie (whom he despises) for the sake of "doing good." Willie seems to have made his point, with Burden's help, that good must be created out of evil—because, Stark says, that is all there is available to make it out of. Even Willie, however, expedient and pragmatic though he is, has a vision of the hospital, which is to be free to anyone in need of medical service, as an unsullied oasis in a grimy world, a monument of his own submerged idealism.

Jack is also due for a moral shock that dislodges the last rosy illusion of his own past. In spite of his cynicism, he has always maintained a vision of Anne as a somehow incorruptible spirit. He still dwells fondly on an Eden-like summer long ago when they were in love and he "nobly" refrained from violating her sexually, as he could have. He never understood why Anne had declined to marry him. When he discovers from an irate Sadie Burke, the boss's secretary and sometime mistress, that Willie is now Anne's lover, Jack flees from such image-shattering knowledge both mentally and physically. He precipitously drives out West until he is stopped in Long Beach by the Pacific Ocean. There he drops into what he calls the "Great Sleep," a neurotic reaction which has afflicted him before—once when he walked out on his Ph.D. studies in history and once when he walked out on his wife.

From the Great Sleep, Jack is born again into a bleak but emotionally insulating belief in the "Great Twitch," an understanding of the world as completely amoral and mechanistic, wherein nobody has any responsibility for what happens. ". . . all life is but the dark heave of the blood and the twitch of the nerve." Encapsulated in this protective nihilism, he returns to his job as if nothing had happened. He thinks he has attained the final wisdom and is now invulnerable to the vagaries of fortune. He hardly hesitates at all when Willie wants to use the evidence against Judge Irwin. But because he had promised Anne that he would confront Irwin with the evidence before delivering it to Stark, Burden goes once more to Irwin's house.

Judge Irwin is shocked by Jack's evidence, not just because an old crime has been discovered but because he had literally forgotten it. He does not deny it, however, and enigmatically suggests that he could prevent Jack from using this evidence, although he does not intend to do so. Not until the next day does the complaisant Burden understand the full irony of Judge Irwin's strange reaction. Burden goes back to his mother's house, not far from Judge Irwin's, and sinks into a deep sleep. He is awakened, literally and figuratively, by his mother's shrill screams. (This, too, is a rebirth into a new truth, but one not calculated to protect him from the world.) His mother is at the telephone and has just been told that Judge Irwin has shot himself. She turns toward Jack the accusing finger and the dreadful charge that he has killed his father.

Jack's icy, but fast-melting shield protects him only a little while longer. When a lawyer calls him to reveal that he is the sole heir to Judge Irwin's estate, Jack breaks at last, first into desperate laughter, and then tears, moaning, "The poor old bugger, the poor old bugger. It was like the ice breaking up after a long winter."

Burden's education in tragedy is not yet complete, however. He witnesses a curious reversal of the father-son relationship when Willie Stark becomes indirectly responsible for his own son Tom's death. Burden had suffered psychologically from a seeming neglect by his father—both his supposed parent (cynically called the "Scholarly Attorney") who deserted his mother, and his real father, Judge Irwin, who never acknowledged his paternity. Tom Stark, however, suffers from too much attention from Willie. Like many a common man who has scrabbled up the social ladder the hard way, Willie wants his son to taste the success and advantages he once craved. Against the wishes of Tom's sensible mother, Lucy, Willie pushes Tom to become a college football hero, lavishes praise on him, and unintentionally creates a vain and selfish young man. Willie reaps some of the reward for such misguided parenting when his political enemies threaten a paternity suit, using one of Tom's sleazy girlfriends, who is pregnant. But the final blow comes when Tom breaks his neck in a football game. Tom is left paralyzed thereby and eventually dies, though not until Willie has met his own nemesis.

Adam Stanton is tipped off by an anonymous telephone call that his sister is Willie's mistress and given to understand that this was the reason for Adam's appointment as director. One truth, one lie—together they are enough to break Adam's brittle shell of control. Adam goes berserk, shoots Willie at close range, and is himself riddled with bullets by Willie's faithful driver, Sugar-Boy O'Sheean.

Jack Burden, still the searcher for truth, discovers that the telephone caller had been Tiny Duffy, although Sadie Burke had leaked the fatal information about the Willie-Anne affair. Tiny Duffy has succeeded Willie as governor of the state. When Jack meets Sugar-Boy again, he is tempted to recreate the crime by revealing to Sugar-Boy the fact of Tiny's guilt. Burden knows that Sugar-Boy would shoot Tiny as surely as Adam destroyed Willie, and he, Jack, would be legally untouchable, just as Tiny is now. But he does not take the opportunity, for he realizes now the complexity of guilt that envelops him in all that has happened—and the fact that an act of vengeance is never the end of any story.

All the King's Men, more complex than *Night Rider* and philosophically more balanced and "just" than *At Heaven's Gate*, remains Warren's literary masterpiece, never quite equaled in subsequent novels. Plot, theme, and point of view keep everything perfectly interrelated, even the "story within the story" of Cass Mastern, the problem of history that led Burden to flee graduate school.

Burden could not understand the pervasive guilt that dogs Cass Mastern all his life after having had an affair with a friend's wife, which led to his friend's suicide and the wife's heartless selling of her personal slave down the river. This story, which Warren has dramatized in a play also, repeats the elements of betrayal and adultery that permeate the main plot. Each seemingly private sin has unforseen repercussions in society.

As a matter of fact, though both Willie Stark and Judge Irwin might be accused of public crimes, it was their private adulteries that destroyed them. And Adam Stanton's private sense of honor was expressed as a politically significant murder. And Jack Burden had, through his passivity and noninvolvement, virtually handed over Anne Stanton to his more dynamic boss and thus set the stage for assassination. Perhaps the only equally well-known novel that has so convincingly dramatized the interconnected, communal nature of human guilt is Dostoevsky's *The Brothers Karamazov*. In the final analysis, all are guilty, and each man brings about his own destruction.

However, the universality of guilt in the novel is not exactly a religious sentiment but rather a more subtle observation of a symbiotic psychological dependency between people. No one is complete and self-sufficient, not even Anne, although the narrator early in the book assumes that she is peculiarly integrated and whole. Anne actually shares with Jack an essential passivity that makes them both feed emotionally on the dynamic energy of Willie Stark.

The gravitation of the passive personality to the active man also has its political expression, accounting for the success of the demagogue with his constituents, who feel themselves to be socially and politically helpless. He is probably more significant as an antidote to their depression than as an answer to their physical needs.

The most striking symbiotic relationship in the novel, however, is that between Willie Stark and Adam Stanton.

As a student of history, Jack Burden could see that Adam Stanton, whom he came to call the man of idea, and Willie Stark, whom he came to call the man of fact, were doomed to destroy each other, just as each was doomed to try to become the other, because each was incomplete with the terrible division of their age.

This equation of the opposition between Adam and Willie with the "division of their age" universalizes the situation, suggesting that such private dilemmas are a reflection of the state of society, a society in which idealism and practical action are often poles apart. The novel raises more questions, perhaps, than it can answer—perhaps more than anyone can answer. Surely no one is satisfied with the nature of politics. Even that considerable wisdom and reconciliation Burden attains by the end of the novel does not quite blot out his cynical argument with the Scholarly Attorney-turned-evangelist:

"Politics is action and all action is but a flaw in the perfection of inaction, which is peace, just as all being is but a flaw in the perfection of non-being. Which is God . . . Then God is nothing."

This passage has more than a touch of oriental mysticism, suggesting the principle of "wu wei" (inaction) in the Book of Tao, but its definition of God as nothingness is modern and existential in effect—a difference in tone, since the Taoist "inaction" is not perceived in this skeptical, bitter way. Perhaps the error in the idea expressed is the way Burden, at this point in the novel, makes use of it to repudiate responsibility. As Sartre or any other existentialist would maintain, even the refusal to choose is a choice, and the avoidance of action is an act for which one must bear responsibility. The absence of intrinsic or absolute moral meaning in human action does not mean that action is without moral content. Willie Stark was perhaps more to the point when he suggested that good must be created out of evil. He too, of course, misuses whatever truth there may be in that position by perverting the principle to justify political expediency.

The kind of ambiguity that may be contained in half-truths or even outright lies is dramatized in Burden's parting with his mother. She asks Jack if Monty (Judge Irwin) was in any trouble that would account for his suicide. Jack lies, affirming the "official version," that the Judge was in bad health—not to protect himself from blame but to protect her memory of the man she had always loved and her already considerable burden of guilt. She has apparently repressed her initial stark intuition that Jack had killed his father. One is reminded of the ending of *Heart of Darkness*, where the enlightened Marlowe lies to Kurtz's betrothed, maintaining her illusions about her lover's goodness. The truth would have been "too dark altogether." Burden does not want his mother to drown by trying to climb out of the sustaining sea of ideas.

The clearer instance, however, of creating good out of evil, or truth out of lies, is the reconciliation of Lucy Stark to the disasters that surround her. Lucy has been the victim in all the action—the betrayed wife, the frustrated mother, the simple person of natural rectitude who can only suffer the world's reality. Yet she, more than any other, finds a way to survive, a way even to survive with joy. She has chosen, not in ignorance but with a pure act of the will, to adopt "Tom's baby," knowing full well that its parentage is unknowable. She demonstrates the possibility of "created good" and "chosen truth." Willie, she affirms, was a great man, and this child is their grandson. Situational ethics has here achieved a moral victory that neither Willie Stark nor Adam Stanton could attain. Her example helps, perhaps, the other survivors, Jack and Anne, to live through their more precarious and guilt-laden reconciliation with the past.

The problem of creating good out of evil has a related difficulty, which the novel also explores: How can one make a new self when all we have to make it with is the old self? We have seen how Burden tries repeatedly to be born again in the light of some (usually inadequate) knowledge he has acquired. At one point he quite accurately defines the problem of self-knowledge in this way: ". . . by the time we understand the pattern we are in, the definition we are making for ourselves, it is too late to break out of the box. We can only live in terms of the definition, like the prisoner in the cage in which he cannot lie or stand or sit, hung up in justice to be viewed by the populace." This sounds very like the medieval dungeon, called "the house of little ease," where one can neither sit nor lie down nor stand erect, which Albert Camus's narrator in *The Fall* describes as the human condition. An ironic commentary on the principle of one's self as a cage occurs late in the novel, when Adam allows Jack to witness a prefrontal lobotomy, the one dependable way science has found to change personality. Though this violent method of changing people seems almost ludicrously crude, Adam does have some idea what must or should happen if people are to change.

World Enough and Time (1950)

> Had we but World enough and time,
> This coyness Lady were no crime.
> We would sit down, and think which way
> To walk, and pass our long Loves Day.

Marvell's sly mockery of romantic pretensions in a fleeting world suggests, but does not exhaust, Warren's examination of love's long day—a day too long, perhaps too agonizingly protracted beyond Love's fitful climax and humiliating decline. The nature of love is not the only issue here, however, but that other, less sentimental, concept called justice and its imagined entourage of honor and nobility. "I had longed for some nobility . . ." explains Jeremiah Beaumont, who murdered his benefactor, presumably to avenge a gross insult to his wife. "Was all for naught?"

Seldom have human aspirations been so relentlessly exposed, one after another, as frail illusions. One has the impression that the author, though trying to speak the truth (another one of those glorious human abstractions) is lacerating his own heart and his own persistent desire to believe in love and justice and honor against all evidence to the contrary. This ambiguous double vision of the subjective preference for illusion, coupled with the hard drive for objective truth, is certainly deliberate in that it is appropriate to his protagonist. One should not assume, of course, that an author shares the perceptions of the character he creates. Nonetheless, the tortured passions of this "romance" seem to burn closer to Warren's "real hell" than the more objective inferno in *At Heaven's Gate*.

Though it might be termed a historical novel, since it is based loosely on an actual event, or a philosophical novel, since it comments repeatedly on the abstract meaning of human behavior and aspiration, *World Enough and Time* is better termed a psychological novel or, more precisely perhaps, an examination of the psychological motivations for philosophizing. It is certainly not, like Marvell's poem, a neat argument for seizing our pleasures while we may. It is not a neat argument for any philosophical position, actually, but it illuminates the sequential confusion of a reasonably thoughtful, well-meaning person trying to identify himself and justify his actions.

Jeremiah Beaumont, the orphaned son of an unsuccessful Kentucky farmer in the early nineteenth century, acquires a better than average education by becoming the protégé of a country doctor named Dr. Burnham.

Burnham is a grossly fat man and as medically incompetent as most doctors were in that time and place, but he
respects learning and instructs young Jerry as though he
were his own son. Moreover, Burnham advances Jeremiah's expectations by recommending him to his good
friend Colonel Cassius Fort, a well-known lawyer and
statesman of the region. Colonel Fort, like Dr. Burnham,
treats Jeremiah like a son and gives him a thorough
grounding in the law.

To the idealistic young Beaumont, Colonel Fort
is a living legend. Jeremiah writes in his journal that
Fort really *was* the "son of old Kaintuck," the
"border brawler," the "humorist," "soldier," "gentleman of honor," "lawyer and statesman bearing the fate of
the people," the "retired student who read poetry without
apology or discussed the philosophy of Voltaire and
Hume without shame." But his face has about it the look
"of a suffering animal that has no words for what it feels."

Beaumont's exalted view of his mentor receives a
cruel blow from Jerry's dashing friend, Wilkie Barron, a
popular man-about-town and a dabbler in politics—a
kind of Steerforth to Jerry's David Copperfield. Wilkie
tells him of a beautiful woman he once loved in vain, who
was seduced by an older man who came to console her
when her father died. The young lady in question, Rachel
Jordan, had a child, born dead, and the villain had no
more to do with her. And who was the knave who wronged
her but the unimpeachable Colonel Fort!

The persuasive Wilkie succeeds in promoting in a
somewhat passive Jerry a romantic vision of wronged
womanhood. From this point on, Jerry creates his own
drama of love and revenge, though Wilkie continues to
manipulate him in ways he never understands until near
the end of his life. Jeremiah repudiates Colonel Fort and
woos and at last wins the lovely 'Rachel, who is in a
neurotic state of depression, not because of the perfidy of
Colonel Fort but because of her baby's death. Jeremiah,

blind to the true source of her despondency, hounds her into commanding him to kill Fort to defend her honor. Fort refuses to duel with Jerry, however, and the honorable vengeance seems destined to fizzle out. Rachel is pregnant, and Jerry is fitting into the comfortable role of country squire, even running (unsuccessfully) for public office at Wilkie's urging. Then an unknown messenger brings to Rachel an infamous handbill in which Colonel Fort, presumably combating an expose by his political opponents about his affair with Rachel, claims that Rachel had taken a slave to her bed. Fort had claimed paternity to the child as a chivalric gesture. This shocking message precipitates Rachel's labor, and Jeremiah's child is also born dead. Jerry, in remorse, kills Fort—not openly in a duel as he had planned, but secretly, letting it appear to be a political assassination.

Beaumont stands trial, confident that he will be exonerated, for he thinks he has planned his action perfectly. The long trial, however, is a bewildering process in which lies and truths become inextricably mixed. Then his "friend" Wilkie appears and reveals Beaumont's vow to kill Fort, the reaction Wilkie had himself orchestrated even before Jeremiah had met the wronged lady. All is lost: Beaumont awaits hanging. Rachel comes and stays with him in his basement jail cell, where they indulge in a passionate interlude—a veritable frenzy of love in the face of imminent death. (Was Warren thinking again of Marvell's poem with its advice to ". . . tear our Pleasures with rough strife,/Through the Iron gates of Life./Thus, though we cannot make our Sun/Stand still, yet we will make him run"?) Rachel swears she will kill herself when Jerry dies.

The reappearance of Dr. Burnham, now an old man almost immobilized in an even more monstrous burden of flesh, offers the chance for a new drama, a death more dignified than the gallows. Jerry begs the doctor to provide him with poison for himself and Rachel. But the

romance of the double suicide deteriorates into the most
wretched fiasco. There is so much laudanum in the bottle
from which they drink that it acts as an emetic, forcing
the uncontrolled expulsion of the poison by vomiting and
diarrhea. Before Jeremiah and Rachel have recovered
from the abortive suicide attempt, the unpredictable
Wilkie appears with his men, overpowers the guards,
and rescues the two out of the prison. Wilkie sends them
out West with a backwoodsman to live in the desolate
island refuge of a notorious bandit.

This is a return to nature, akin to Jack Burden's big
sleep and Munn's flight to escape prosecution, but a
nature devoid of its original innocence, incapable of
healing the scars of "civilization." Jerry sinks into an
almost bestial pattern, and Rachel begins to lose her
sanity. Beaumont learns from the ruffian who led them to
this dreary haven that Wilkie forged the infamous
handbill that induced Rachel's miscarriage and Jeremiah's murder of Fort. Jerry feels betrayed by everyone
he has ever known. Rachel kills herself in a passion of
despair. Beaumont is murdered as he seeks to find his
way back to the hangman, resigned now to the most
austere prize of all—neither love nor honor but simply
knowledge. There is no particular assurance, even at this
point, however, that his bitter knowledge is the same as
wisdom.

The failure of the suicide pact and the subsequent
escape to an even greater horror seem a pernicious
extension of suffering, though they serve a thematic
purpose. Warren strains somewhat at the message that
dreams *never* come true. This portion of the tale has no
historical reference, by the way, since the real Jeroboam
Beauchamp, who murdered Col. Solomon Sharp in 1825,
hanged on schedule. The real trial and the deaths of
Beauchamp and his wife, Ann Cook, were only slightly
less miserable than Warren's fictional denouement.
According to a 1950 review by Malcolm Cowley:

After a long trial that was complicated by political issues and confused by perjury on both sides, Beauchamp was sentenced to be hanged. . . . On the night before the execution Ann joined him in his cell and they drank what they thought would be a fatal draught of laudanum; it failed to kill them and they stabbed themselves. Ann died, but Beauchamp survived his wound to die on the scaffold.[1]

Warren's fictional extension to allow further demoralization of the lovers does help to explore all possible approaches to the problem of reconciling the ideal and the real, sometimes stated as the idea and the world, or again, in Biblical language, as the Word made flesh. At first, Jeremiah thought that the idea must redeem the world. Idea is all, he thought, and quoted John Locke on the piece of gold that, outside our world, would have no color, no weight, no value. The mental context defines the object. But this route led to an idealism divorced from action, and allowed a further evil to develop in the world, the death of his child. Then he thought the world would redeem the idea, that is, the act of killing Fort would vindicate the idea of honor. Then in his flight to the West, he commits a third error, the opposite to his first: to deny the idea completely and embrace the world as "to seek communion only in the blank cup of nature." Perhaps this tortured journey through innocence and experience should lead to some Blakean reconciliation of opposites, but if so, that too seems more dream than reality. "There must be a way whereby the word becomes flesh," muses Jeremiah in his last days. But "I no longer seek to justify. I seek only to suffer." If this is not a particularly lucid analysis of philosophical possibilities, it may nevertheless be psychologically true to the mental and moral confusion in which men live. Perhaps it is intended to represent that "terror of the awakening" Warren speaks of in Conrad's *Lord Jim* when the "hero recognizes the terms on which he may be saved. . . ."

Malcolm Cowley has analyzed perceptively the

striking complexity of the plot of this novel. He claims that
the whole is too rich to be completely digestible,
containing four quite different novels combined into one.
The first is historical and romantic: "a story of love and
revenge, of murders, seductions, treacheries, and jail
deliveries." The second is political: "a struggle between
debtors and creditors in pioneer Kentucky . . . to discover
the different conceptions of justice that lie behind all
political struggles. . . ." The third is realistic and
psychological, with an undertone of irony: "the portrait of
a self-deluded romanticist" whose crime ruined not only
his own life but also that of the woman whose honor he
defended. The other novel Malcolm calls a myth of
extended parable, wherein Beaumont is the "dupe in a
political struggle"; his crime is parricide and the story is
the struggle of everyman back to "moral consciousness."[2]
This analysis certainly illuminates the remarkable, but
somewhat confusing, impact of the story.

The style of the novel sometimes has a lyrical, poetic
quality, especially the early part of it in which the young
Jerry is struggling with his first disillusionments, his first
impressions of the "blindness of man's fate." A hellfire-
and-brimstone evangelist, Corinthian McClardy, is
working the territory, and the description of the Kentucky
landscape does much to account for the necessity of
illusion, whether religious or romantic, in men's lives:

August is hot in South Kentucky, the corn is laid by, and in that
moment between full effort and harvest there is an interlude of
sad idleness in which a man knows that another year is spent and
that even if the year is a good year at last, the biggest heap of
full-grained ears and the whisky-fun of the corn-husking party
will not quite bleach out the stain of vanity from all his labors or
fulfill some promise which had seemed to be made long back.
Scum gathers on ponds, the water is brackish in the well, the cow
goes dry, tempers are short, the husband notices that his old wife
has lost her teeth and sags in the tits, the young man had rather
cut the guts out of a friend with a dirk than tumble a juicy girl

back of the old mill, and all the old meaning of life is lost like water spilled in the ankle-deep dust. The sun boils down all day every day, and at night the Dog Star is baleful and the moon rises the color of blood. It was the right season for Corinthian McClardy, and he knew how to evoke the last wild energy left from aimlessness and unrecognized despair. "Many lay on the ground before him, and many were saved."

Jeremiah knew the terror but he could not be saved. He saw those who were saved and "hated them for their salvation." They had some gift they could bring to God and get His mercy, but he, Jeremiah Beaumont, had nothing in hand to offer for the price of his soul.

This passage brings to mind José Ortega y Gasset's *Meditations on Quixote*, in which he explains the relationship between Don Quixote's fantasy and the real nature of the setting of La Mancha:

In summer the sun pours down torrents of fire on La Mancha, and frequently the burning earth produces the effect of a mirage. The water which we see is not real water, but there is something real in it: its source. This bitter source, which produces the water of the mirage, is the desperate dryness of the land. We can experience a similar phenomenon in two directions; one simple and straight, seeing the water which the sun depicts as actual; another ironic, oblique, seeing it as a mirage, that is to say, seeing through the coolness of the water the dryness of the earth in disguise. The ingenuous manner of experiencing imaginary and significant things is found in the novel of adventure, the tale, the epic; the oblique manner in the realistic novel. The latter needs the mirage to make us see it as such. So it is not only that *Quixote* was written against the books of chivalry, and as a result bears them within it, but that the novel as a literary genre consists essentially of such an absorption.[3]

World Enough and Time is a realistic novel in the way Ortega suggests, offering an oblique, ironic view of "imaginary and significant things." Yet there is a difference in effect. Perhaps the *significance* of those imaginary things is more solid in Warren's view, and the barrenness of human life without love and justice makes the mirage indispensable. Jeremiah, like many of us, cannot subside gently into Christian assurances of justice and love hereafter, like Cervantes's disenchanted knight. These issues, whether real or imaginary, are here and now and part of the unsubstantial fabric of our lives.

Quite aside from the philosophical burden of the novel, Warren uses a number of literary devices with considerable skill. Throughout this long and eventful novel, for instance, there is nearly always an element of suspense and surprise. The reader, like the protagonist, suffers one revelation after another, yet there is always some unrevealed mystery.

The careful pacing of these disclosures matches the repeated motif of death and rebirth, a pattern we have seen before in *All the King's Men* and elsewhere. Jeremiah awakens to some new insight periodically, even though it is like awakening from one dream into another. Sooner or later the new truth is modified in the light of further revelation. In spite of Jerry's skepticism in the early episode about the evangelist McClardy, for instance, he does experience a conversion—or at least a hysterical seizure of some sort at a religious tent meeting—after which he flees madly into the forest. The religious quality of this experience is immediately compromised by his sexual assault on a lone woman he stumbles over in the woods. This is his first sexual experience. When the hysteria is dissipated, he finds himself in "the embrace of a snaggle-toothed hag whose hair was snarled and greasy against his face and whose odor offended his nostrils." He flees from her with "the horror of contamination and betrayal." Afterwards he immerses himself repeatedly in the cold water of the river. The ritual suggests religious baptism, certainly, and literally an attempt to decontaminate himself, but he emerges from this baptism permanently cured of Christianity.

The old woman in the woods is a symbolic figure, much like the Jungian anima, which recurs from time to time in other guises. Jeremiah fancies he sees her again in the vindictive face of Rachel's ailing mother, who spies on him from the shadows but never comes forward to meet him openly. He marries Rachel only after the old woman dies. Sometimes Rachel herself suggests this mythic figure, like "La Belle Dame Sans Merci," now hag, now siren. This is in Jeremiah's fancy, for Rachel never plays the siren, actually, but is a somewhat unwilling participant in his dream. Jerry meets a younger but no less unsavory version of the hag in the sodden outlaw community in the wilderness. He rolls with her in drunken debauchery, even as the demented Rachel steals the slut's unwanted baby and croons over it as her own.

Another familiar pattern in this novel is the cluster of father-son relationships. Jeremiah has even more fathers or pseudofathers than Jack Burden. Jerry's attitude toward his real father, who dies leaving his mother to struggle on in dire poverty, is a combination of shame and defensiveness. The maternal grandfather, who despised the elder Beaumont, wanted to adopt Jeremiah but threw him out when Jerry refused to change his name from his father's to his grandfather's. Dr. Burnham and Cassius Fort were both fathers to the orphaned boy. Each of these older men, like the old uncle with the wen in "Original Sin," bears the mark of the fallen adult world, Fort with his sad animal face and Burnham with his mountain of flesh. But the most hideous of Jeremiah's surrogate fathers is *La Grande Bosse* (The Great Hump), the aged, humpbacked river pirate who tyrannizes the wilderness settlement. He is sheer bestiality, deprived of the beauty of wild beasts. His is the gray-faced baby in filthy rags that Rachel clutches to her starved bosom, and his is the swarthy slut that Jeremiah sports with—a hideous reenactment of Jerry's original inheritance of Cassius Fort's mistress.

In spite of its sometimes melodramatic turn of the screw (in both the metaphorical and obscene sense of that term), *World Enough and Time* brings the past alive through Warren's sure command of dialogue, characterization, and action and his intimate understanding of Kentucky backgrounds. The symbolic geography of the psycho-drama is perhaps more personal to the author than to the crime and punishment recorded in history; yet its implications of universality are legitimate. The conflicts between the ideal and the real have not died with the posturings of nineteenth-century Romanticism.

4

The Once and Future Self: Poetry, 1953–1975

> To wake in some dawn and see
> As though down a rifle barrel, lined up
> Like sights, the self that was, the self that is,
>   and there,
> Far off but in range, completing that alignment,
>   your fate.
>
> —"Audubon"

Brother to Dragons

Warren emerged from his prose-only period as a poet of peculiar power and originality with the publication in 1953 of *Brother to Dragons*, sometimes called the most successful long poem in American literature. He has recently (1979) brought out a revised edition, which has a few cuts from the original and some additions. Warren has made some changes in rhythm and has expanded somewhat the role of Meriwether Lewis, who came West on the Lewis and Clark expedition. Meriwether was a cousin to Lilburne Lewis, the murderer, and a special favorite of their kinsman Thomas Jefferson. For some reason unknown to me, Warren has changed the name of the murdered slave from George in the first version to John in the later one. Perhaps John seemed the more neutral and universal name. John is purely a victim, not only the victim of one man's neurotic (or psychotic) destructiveness but also a representative victim of the social evil of slavery and unwitting participant in an even more universal human psychodrama of good and evil. For general readers, the difference between the two versions is probably not significant. I shall use the 1979 edition for this discussion, trusting to the author's judgment that it is the version he prefers.

Warren invented a unique mode of presentation for this remarkable work—neither narrative poem nor play, but a discussion by characters long dead (except for one, the poet himself, RPW), who try to understand the grisly event that occurred in the meat house when Lilburne Lewis hacked to pieces a teenage slave because he broke a pitcher belonging to Lucy Jefferson Lewis, Lilburne's deceased mother. As Warren explains in a brief preface: "We may take them to appear and disappear as their urgencies of argument swell and subside. The place of this meeting is, we may say, 'no place,' and the time is 'any time.'" Besides John, the murdered slave, the characters include Lilburne; Isham Lewis, who watched his older brother commit the murder; their mother, Lucy; her brother, Thomas Jefferson; Letitia, Lilburne's wife; Aunt Cat, a slave and Lilburne's Negro mammy; Meriwether; and RPW. Lilburne's father, Charles, and Letitia's brother have minor roles.

The central character, if the poem can be said to have one, is not the hapless victim, who has only one brief speech in the first edition and three in the revision. It is not even Lilburne, the moral monster, but Thomas Jefferson, inheritor of eighteenth-century optimism about the perfectibility of man. The poem examines the hideous events and ponders why it occurred, but it is Jefferson who develops and changes in the poem. There is no evidence that the historical Thomas Jefferson ever discussed or even acknowledged the murder, a fact which suggested to Warren that he could not face the thought of such barbarity in one of his own blood.

Actually, the stance of Jefferson in the poem is initially very grim and cynical. He has already recognized that he had been overly optimistic in his view of human nature. The moral project of the poem is not to convince Jefferson of the reality of evil, which he affirms from the first, but to convince him that he himself shares that burden of human evil. This humbling of Jefferson is achieved primarily by burdening him with some guilt for the fate of Meriwether Lewis, who had once been his secretary. Jefferson ultimately achieves some kind of universalized fellow-feeling, which includes even the despised Lilburne.

Meriwether claims that he tried to live the "lie" (of human goodness?) that Jefferson taught him. Meriwether was betrayed or falsely accused in some manner when he was governor of the Louisiana Territory, and later committed suicide. This is one of the weakest parts of the poem, for the reader does not know, from the poem itself, what happened. But worse, for the purposes of the story, we cannot understand how Jefferson can be held responsible for Meriwether's misfortunes. Perhaps the role of Meriwether should have been reduced rather than expanded. He strikes me as an interloper in this situation, introduced, perhaps, to reflect the father-son relationship, which receives some attention.

Surely, the logical way to show Jefferson that he shares the evil that he repudiates in Lilburne is to point out that Jefferson held slaves. It is the institution of slavery that allowed a man to treat another as an object, a possession over which he has absolute rights. Yet the generalized burden of blame for slavery never seems to be an issue, or if it is, it is considerably muffled.

The slight expansion of the part of John does not really work either as a device to soften the self-righteousness of Jefferson. John's original speech is indeed appropriate:

> I was lost in the world, and the trees were tall.
> I was lost in the world and the dark swale heaved.
> I was lost in my anguish and did not know the reason.

But in this version John also seconds Lucy's plea to her brother, Jefferson, to touch Lilburne:

John: Yes—now is the time—That's all I,
In my ignorance, know.

When Jefferson still refuses, John adds, "Oh, please!"
What possible motivation can poor John have to play this
ameliorative role? These characters are not angels purged
of their earthly faults and possessed of divine wisdom.
What does John have to do with winning compassion for
this bloody murderer? He does not make a convincing
Christ figure, one who would think, even long afterward,
"Forgive them, for they know not what they do."

Because so much of this poem *is* moving and eloquent,
the latter part of it, especially the moralizing to reconcile
Jefferson to the human race, seems unworthy of the drama
that precedes it. Even allowing that Jefferson's encourage-
ment of Meriwether Lewis to become some kind of light-
bringer to the West contributed to whatever evils resulted
from that project, surely Jefferson's good intention has
little resemblance morally to Lilburne's "good" intention
of defending his mother's spoons and dishes. Warren
establishes Lilburne's character not only as mother-fixated
in some neurotic way but also as cruel to everyone who
loved him—his brother, his father, his wife, his Negro
mammy, even his adoring hound. Lilburne forces his wife
into some unspecified sadistic sex act, then holds her in
contempt because she may have enjoyed it. This implication of masochistic tendencies in the victim is curiously
introduced by RPW as a possible suggestion of similar
tendencies in the murder victim. Now, to imply that a
murdered person is in some measure responsible for his
own fate is sometimes perfectly appropriate (consider the
degenerate father of *The Brothers Karamazov*, who earned
hatred from all his sons). But the slave John has not
earned any punishment, at least not in the poem. He was
deliberately set up by Lilburne to be an object lesson to all
the slaves. Lilburne may even have "helped" him to break
the pitcher to create an excuse for his extermination.

In spite of these difficulties with the moral assumptions of the poem, the discussion and the narrated action of the first hundred pages is gripping, both mentally and emotionally. At the psychological level, Warren suggests that the act of murder was a ritualized attempt to purge Lilburne's own evil. John is Lilburne's shadow-self, the scapegoat whose elimination will bring order in a chaotic world or in Lilburne's chaotic psyche. The butcher block, on which John lies curled in the fetal position with eyes tight closed, suggests an altar to some savage god. The death of Lilburne repeats the psychological ritual with Lilburne playing the victim, the dark shadow of his brother Isham. Lilburne forces Isham into a suicide pact, whereby they will shoot each other over their mother's grave. He counts to ten very slowly, knowing full well that Isham will panic and shoot first, then try to escape. Lilburne also acts as Jefferson's shadow-self, acting out the violence that Jefferson has so effectively repressed.

Some of the preliminary images in the poem also suggest an interrelatedness of good and evil. RPW visits the site of the Lewis house in Kentucky. The place has long since burned down. It is overgrown with vegetation, but some stone ruins remain. A great black snake emerges from the ruins, rearing up over the poet's head like some terrible pagan god.

> In some deep aperture among the stones,
> I saw the eyes, their glitter in that dark,
> And suddenly the head thrust forth, and the fat, black,
> Body, molten, out-flowed, as though those stones
> Bled forth earth's inner darkness to the day—
> As though the bung had broke on that intolerable
> inwardness.
> Thus, now divulged, focused, and compacted,
> The thing that haunts beneath earth's soldered sill
> Flowed forth, and the scaled belly of abomination
> Rustled on stone, reared up
> In regal indolence and swag.

> I saw the soiled white of belly bulge,
> And in that muscular distension, the black side scales
> Show their faint yellow flange and tracery of white.
> It climbed the paralyzed light.

RPW, although understandably shaken by this portentous form, quickly assures us that it was a harmless mountain black snake, good for killing rats, "no spirit, symbol, god,/Or Freudian principle, but just a snake." After the poet's deliberate demythologizing of the snake as symbol of evil, the beast seems more humble:

> . . . the head
> Wagged slow, benevolent and sad and sage,
> As though it understood our human limitation
> And forgave all, and asked forgiveness, too.

This image of the morally ambiguous snake follows by a page or two a marvelous extended metaphor about virtue as a praying mantis:

> You know that virtue, painful as a syllogism,
> Waits, and will wait, as on
> The leaf the lethal mantis at his prayer,
> And under those great hands, spiked, Gothic, barbed,
> Clasped high to arch the summer blue of heaven,
> You pass, like ant or aphid in the season's joy, while he,
> That green, crank nightmare of the dear green world,
> All day, in sun and shade, maintains
> His murderous devotion.
> For you will come and under the barbed arch meet
> The irremediable logic of all the anguish
> Your cunning could invent or heart devise.
> Or is any answer as complete as that?
>
> Who has seen man in his naked absoluteness?

The implication is that virtue, with its pseudoreligious devotion, may be just as savage as the maligned snake. They both suggest that good and evil are not so neatly separated as moralists would like to think.

No matter what the thematic difficulties of the poem,

it was a courageous work to come from the pen of a Southerner in 1953, showing the white slave owner in his worst possible light and suggesting at the same time that even our most respected founding fathers were not without sin. Well, Mr. Warren, would you consider writing a novel about Jefferson and his slave mistress, by whom he had several children? That should be good for a few poignant paradoxes. I wonder about the identity problems of the child of an American president, framer of the Declaration of Independence, and a black slave. Think of the possibilities—one could show Jefferson both as chief hypocrite and as true believer in human equality!

Other Poetry

Warren's unique method in *Brother to Dragons*, a "tale in verse and voices," is not radically different from many of his other sets of poems. Warren's usual method of organization is to write a series of poems exploring elements in a topic; the sequence is like a symphony, composed of separate movements. The thematic connection between the poems is sometimes tenuous, but some series are tightly knit.

The five-part sequence entitled "Mortmain" in *You, Emperors and Others*, for instance, is one of those closely related series, exploring the struggle to understand the relationship between the persona and his father, who has recently died. ("Mortmain" means the influence of the past as it controls the present.) The persona in these poems seems hardly distinguishable from Warren himself, since the events follow closely the facts of his father's life and the kind of guilt feeling which Warren has expressed in conversation. Each movement is dated, beginning with the deathbed scene (1955); the father's past (1885); the persona's present (1956), remembering his past; a meditation marked N.D. (no date); and a vision of his father as a young boy (1880).

What is achieved in the process is not so much an understanding of causes and effects in any linear manner easily explained, but rather an interpretation of past, present, and future, existing simultaneously in the consciousness. The continuity of personal history into the future is touched upon briefly in the third poem, where "I hear now my small son laugh from a farther room."

The lengthy title of the first poem presents the problem to the persona, stricken with grief, vague guilt, confusion: "After Night Flight Son Reaches Bedside of Already Unconscious Father, Whose Right Hand Lifts in a Spasmodic Gesture. As Though Trying to Make Contact: 1955." This section is an excellent example of the principle of "impurity" in image and language, which, though seemingly unsuitable for the solemn occasion, makes it a peculiarly wrenching experience.

> In Time's concatenation and
> Carnal conventicle, I
> Arriving, being flung through dark and
> The abstract flight-grid of sky,
> Saw rising from the sweated sheet and
> Ruck of bedclothes ritualistically
> Reordered by the paid hand
> Of mercy—saw rising the hand—

The cynical voice ("paid hand/Of mercy"); the too clever, ambiguous definition of the situation in the first two lines ("Carnal conventicle" suggests something morbid or unlawful in this meeting), and its stagy use of alliteration; the merciless observation of messiness in reality ("sweated sheet," "Ruck of bedclothes")—all invest this event with a painful confusion of emotions and perceptions. The abstract flight through darkness, with its suggestion of idealizing the notion of death, ends with a close view that is all struggle and disorder (in spite of the continual, ritual attempt to hide the truth). The paid hand is opposed to the portentous hand of the father, reaching out to the son even in death.

So devastating is this experience, that the son seeks to fend off the anguish of it with flippant, childish formulations—"opp-si daisy . . . daddio's got/One more shot in the locker. . . ." The final stanza, however, strips him of all his pretense of distance, sophistication, and cyncism, leading to a final line of stark agony:

> But no. Like an eyelid the hand sank, strove
> Downward, and in that darkening roar,
> All things—all joy and the hope that strove,
> The failed exam, the admired endeavor,
> Prizes and prinkings, and the truth that strove,
> And back of the Capitol, boyhood's first whore—
> Were snatched from me, and I could not move,
> Naked in that black blast of his love.

The second section has the ambiguous title "A Dead Language: Circa 1885," referring indirectly to the son's trying to understand his father's past experience. It concerns the events noted in the biographical chapter of this book, wherein Warren's father gave up serious pursuit of an intellectual career to become a businessman in order to fulfill his obligations to an extended family. The father's knowledge of Greek, the "dead language" of the title, serves as a symbol of what the father relinquished. He speaks to his young son in Greek, as he is shaving:

> "That's Greek, now you know how it sounds!"
> And laughed, and waved the bright blade like a toy.
> And laughing from the deep of a dark conquest and joy,
> Said: "Greek—but it wasn't for me. Let's get to breakfast,
> boy.".

Both the sinister razor, here so gaily wielded as though to amputate a part of the self no longer needed, and the dead language become emblematic of his father's peculiar victory over necessity. The razor image returns later, like a leitmotif in music, in a different, though related context: "Hope dances on the razor edge." Although the knowl-

edge of Greek had little practical application to his life as
a businessman, the father bequeathed the passion of
learning to his son. But more than this, he demonstrated
a capacity for joyful sacrifice of his early dream. It is this
emotional triumph over circumstances that fascinates
the son, now grown. The son feels vaguely guilty for
having lived his father's dream, yet the father's joy
makes his son's guilt seem absurd and useless.

The third movement, entitled "Fox-Fire: 1956,"
struggles to put these warring feelings into some rational
perspective. He has found his father's old Greek grammar text.

> . . . There must be a way to state the problem.
> The statement of a problem no doubt, determines solu-
>   tion.
> If once, clear and distinct, I could state it, then God
> Could no longer fall back on His old alibi of ignorance.
> I hear now my small son laugh from a farther room.

The speaker's son, still innocent, considers his bright-
colored toys as "images . . . of Life's significance."
Unable to cope with the contradictions of perception, the
poet gives up the task, at last, simply placing his father's
Greek grammar beside the one from which he himself
learned Greek some thirty years ago. What began as a
problem which ought to be statable in rational terms
ends in a vivid play of imagination, still rife with
contradiction:

> . . . leave the dark room,
> And know that all night, while the constellations grind,
> Beings with folded wings brood above that shelf,
> Awe-struck and imbecile, and in the dark,
> Amid History's vice and vacuity, that poor book burns
> Like fox-fire in the black swamp of the world's error.

A cacophony of meanings makes the passage taut. There
are angel presences, but they are imbecile. The "poor
Book," which represents his father's devotion to seem-

ingly irrelevant learning, is inexplicable in a pragmatic world. Its radiance seems to be a trick of light, an illusion.

Perhaps it would be fruitful to compare the passage with a more famous one by Shakespeare, where the poet takes the ugliest reality (a drowned man's body—though, ironically, the character has not really drowned, but his son thinks he has), and transforms such a horror into the most beautiful illusion: "Full fathom five thy father lies./ Of his bones are coral made./Those are pearls that were his eyes," and so on—a touchstone in the triumph of the imagination over the most sickening actuality. But Warren's persona, like Warren himself, keeps one foot firmly planted in the earth-knowledge of Caliban, and cannot, therefore, achieve such transformation. Yet, the next section, "In the Turpitude of Time: N.D.," which seeks in nature some answer equal to the unstatable question, suggests that perhaps his father had some secret of transformation or a way back to innocence: "In the heart's last kingdom only the old are young."

In the final poem, "A Vision: Circa 1880," the persona, though standing in a dry wasteland himself, has a vision of his father as a young boy, a glimpse of the prelapsarian world.

> . . . I stare
> Down the tube and darkening corridor of Time
> That breaks, like tears, upon that sunlit space,
> And staring, I know who he is, . . .

The image, though presumably of a past time, seems a vague promise for the future as well. The father's past is mystically united, perhaps, to the persona's son in that "farther room," who also inhabits that prelapsarian world. The air of the desolate present, after the smiling boy moves back into the shadow of woods, "freshens to the far favor of rain."

This brief consideration of one of Warren's complex poetic symphonies may suggest why his poetry requires

such careful attention. It will probably never be popular
with masses of readers, any more than Yeats's or T. S.
Eliot's poetry will. But for that small group of enthusiasts
who have kept alive the so-called classics of literature, I
believe some of Warren's poems will endure as among the
best America has ever produced.

Promises: Poems 1954–1956

Warren broke away from his somewhat morose obsession
with evil with his sparkling *Promises*, winner of his first
Pulitzer Prize for poetry. The first five poems of *Promises*
are dedicated to Warren's daughter Rosanna under the
general title, "To a little Girl, One Year Old, in a Ruined
Fortress." The setting is the imposing ruin overlooking
the Mediterranean where Warren and Eleanor lived in
Italy. The poem "Sirocco" is quoted in the biographical
chapter. It establishes a contrast of perception, which is
maintained through the five poems, between the innocence and delight of the child's view of the world and the
darker awareness of the father, who knows the evil and
suffering enacted here, which, of course, still goes on.
Nevertheless, because he participates and marvels at the
child's innocent joy in nature, the speaker becomes
reconciled to the world, believing, or at least praying, that
all can be redeemed.

The second and third poems introduce some of the
human misery existing in this beautiful setting. The
defective child next door has cried all night; she is the result
of an unsuccessful attempt at abortion. The "monster's"
twelve-year-old sister, who is "beautiful like a saint," has
taught the defective child to make the Italian sign for *ciao*.
The speaker, galled at the assumption that suffering and
tragedy has any such simplistic solution, is moved to
metaphysical rebellion, like Ivan Karamazov, who refused
salvation at the price of the suffering of children.

> I come, and her triptych beauty and joy stir hate
> —Is it hate?—in my heart. Fool, doesn't she know that the
>   process
> Is not that joyous or simple, to bless, or unbless,
> The malfeasance of nature or the filth of fate?

The fourth poem, "The Flower," is the climax experience, where the little daughter's joy in a natural ritual dispels the speaker's rebellion against the world's injustice and pain. He is carrying the child up the cliff from the beach, where in the past she has been given a white flower to hold and a blue one for her hair.

> I carry you up the hill.
> In my arms you are still.
> We approach your special place,
> And I am watching your face
> To see the sweet puzzlement grow,
> And then recognition glow.
> Recognition explodes in delight.
> You leap like spray, or like light.
> Despite my arm's tightness,
> You leap in gold-glitter and brightness.
> You leap like a fish-flash in bright air,
> And reach out. Yes, I'm well aware
> That this is the spot, and hour
> For you to demand your flower.

Since it is fall now, the parents are hard put to find a white bloom not sadly browned and drooping, but the child accepts gladly the best one they can find ". . . as though human need/Were not for perfection." The lyrical joy of this hour seems to transfigure time itself:

> Let the future reassess
> All past joy, and past distress,
> Till the last integument
> Of the past shall be rent
> To show how all things bent
> Their energies to that hour
> When you first demanded your flower.

The speaker has achieved a kind of gestalt experience, which transforms time and history. The closing stanzas, lyrical and serene, echo this transcendent perception of nature in concrete terms. The sea gull the speaker describes is white or black according to its background and the direction of light, suggesting that at least some aspects of reality are matters of human perception. Context determines meaning.

> Just once we look back.
> On sunset, a white gull is black.
> It hangs over the mountain crest.
> It hangs on that saffron west.
> It makes its outcry.
> It slides down the sky.
>
> East now, it catches the light.
> Its black has gone again white,
> And over the *rocca's* height
> It gleams in the last light.
>
> Now it sinks from our sight.
> Beyond the cliff is night.
>
> It sank on unruffled wing.
> We hear the sea rustling.

This lyrical passage achieves its elevation by its perfect fusion of realistic imagery with symbolic language and the sensitive use of sound. Color is, as a matter of fact, a property of light, not of the object itself, and perception depends upon the contrast of background. The symbols so delicately incorporated into the natural scene are thoroughly traditional. Even the variations of symbolic significance for a given quality, such as whiteness, for instance, are both literary and natural. In this poem, the whiteness of the flower (as well as the color of blue) are indicative of innocence, the child's world. It is also in the final passage associated with light and, by extension, truth—that is, whatever is beyond innocence and guilt. Warren sometimes, however, uses whiteness to connote the pallor of death, as in the whiteness of bones, or even the seeming malevolence of God or fate, like Melville's white whale. These variant overtones are not mutually exclusive but reflect the sense of unity and mystery of a world in which both black and white may be illusion.

Warren often uses bird's flight for its traditional association with the soul or self. Here, the fact that the bird "slides down the sky" with the setting sun suggests an awareness of death—in this case, serenely acknowledged since the bird sinks "on unruffled wing" and the sea, with its implications of the source of life, is peaceful. In other poems Warren uses the falling bird as symbol of the fall from innocence—in fact, he does so in the first poem dedicated to his son Gabriel. But these variant implications of the fall of birds as symbolic sin or physical death are no more contradictory than the fact that whiteness may suggest both innocence and death. As a matter of fact, the white flower in this poem is tarnished and thus symbolic not so much of innocence as of the ruined innocence of the adult world, which is the best the parents can offer.

The significant change in the rhyme scheme in the above passage helps to produce a musical coda that emphasizes the positive nature of this reconciliation of opposites. The first stanza (a,a,b,b,c,c) is more typical of the rest of the poem, but the repetition of words rhyming with "light" and "white," with the final admission of "night" (like a minor chord in music), echo the exalted meaning of the poem in both sound and sense.

The final poem in this sequence for Rosanna, "Colder Fire," is less intense than "The Flower," a contemplation somewhat removed from the peak experience of the preceding poem. It begins humbly, readmitting, so to speak, the persistent negative. Though the speaker knows that "the heart should be steadfast," he is often helpless to command his own moods.

It rained toward day. The morning came sad and white
With silver of sea-sadness and defection of season.
Our joys and convictions are sure, but in that wan light
We moved—your mother and I—in muteness of spirit past
   logical reason.
Now sun, afternoon, and again summer-glitter on sea.
As you to a bright toy, the heart leaps. The heart unlocks
Joy, though we know, shamefaced, the heart's weather
   should not be
Merely a reflex to a solstice, or sport of some aggrieved
   equinox.

In this somewhat subdued mood, the speaker sits in the
sun with his child on his lap watching the white
butterflies, soon to die, in their "ritual carouse," nature's
assurance of an immortality of the flesh, reflecting, of
course, the father's sense of immortality in his child.

In whisperless carnival, in vehemence of gossamer,
Pale ghosts of pale passions of air, the white wings weave.
In tingle and tangle of arabesque, they mount light, pair by
   pair,
As though that tall light were eternal indeed, not merely
   the summer's reprieve.

You leap on my knee, you exclaim at the sun-stung
   gyration.
And the upper air stirs, as though the vast stillness of sky
Had stirred in its sunlit sleep and made suspiration,
A luxurious languor of breath, as after love, there is a sigh.

Warren achieves a remarkable fusion of thought, passion,
and concrete imagery. Language, thought, and action
interpenetrate to form a vision of spiritual transcendence
without violating or misrepresenting actual human experience, with its reality of pain and death.

   The longer sequence entitled "Promises," dedicated
to Gabriel, is an examination of Warren's childhood
experience, particularly as he came to realize the presence
of evil or the propensity to violence in himself and others.
It is analogous, in some ways, to William Blake's *Songs of*

Innocence and *Songs of Experience*. He reveals this personal story with the realization that his infant son must also follow this path out of paradise into the fallen world. His son's story will be different in detail, of course, but will be part of the same larger truth.

The first poem, "What Was the Promise That Smiled from the Maples at Evening," echoes with the same concern for time, with its inevitable loss of innocence and its destiny in death, searching always for a reconciliation between human aspiration and human history. "And the heels of the fathers click on the concrete, returning,/Each aware of his own unspecified burden, at sun-dip." The elements of whiteness and cold fire appear again. Here the whiteness is spectral and foreboding, a property of night: "In first darkness hydrangeas float white in their spectral precinct./Beneath pale hydrangeas the first firefly utters cold burning."

The act of original sin on the part of the boy is subtly suggested here, not as an act yet, but as a premonition, another gestalt change in perception, when he picks up a bullbat shot down by older boys, who are already "past regret."

> What was the promise when bullbats dizzied the sunset?
> They skimmer and skitter in gold light at great height.
> The guns of big boys on the common go *boom*, past regret.
> Boys shout when the bullbat spins down in that gold light.
> "Too little to shoot"—but next year you'll be a big boy.
> So shout now and pick up the bird—why, that's blood, it is
>   wet.
> Its eyes are still open, your heart in the throat swells like
>   joy.

The color of gold, as in the "gold light" in which the bullbats soar, is associated in the sequence with the paradise world of the child. The boy finds a "Gold Glade" in the heart of the woods, which haunts him for the rest of his life as a vision of paradise. It is again autumn and the boy has already realized the presence of contamination in himself and even in the old grandfather whom he had idolized. Perhaps it is only with this knowledge that he can recognize the dimension of paradise. (One is reminded here of the complex rhythms of Gerard Manley Hopkins.)

> The glade was geometric, circular, gold,
> No brush or weed breaking that bright gold of leaf-fall.
> In the center it stood, absolute and bold
> Beyond any heart-hurt, or eye's grief-fall.
> Gold-massy the beech stood in that gold light-fall.

Court Martial, the longer poem preceding "Gold Glade," is about the child's shocked realization that his beloved grandfather had hanged guerrillas without trial during the Civil War. The child dreads the rage that still burns in the old man's eyes.

> "By God, they deserved it," he said.
> "Don't look at me that way," he said.
> "By God—" and the old eyes glared red.

The shock of recognition and kinship in blood lust rips away what is left of innocence, and the boy must face the ruined world of adult reality.

> I snatched my gaze away.
> I swung to the blazing day.
> Ruined lawn, raw house swam in light.
> The far woods swam in my sight.
> Throbbing, the fields fell away
> Under the blaze of day.

What follows is as gripping an evocation of the archetypal shadow-self as any to be found in literature. Joseph Conrad's secret sharer, who rose spectrally from the sea to haunt the young captain, seems mild and contemplative beside the hideous forms that gather behind the young cavalry officer in the child's vision.

> Calmly then, out of the sky,
> Blotting the sun's blazing eye,
> He rode. He was large in the sky.

Behind, shadow massed, slow, and grew
Like cloud on the sky's summer blue.
Out of that shade-mass he drew.
To the great saddle's sway, he swung,
Not old now, not old now—but young,
Great cavalry boots to the thigh,
No speculation in eye.
Then clotting behind him, and dim,
Clot by clot, from the shadow behind him,
They took shape, enormous in air.
Behind him, enormous, they hung there:

They are the distorted faces of the hanged men, described in appropriate detail ("hairy jaw askew,/ Tongue out, out-staring eye, . . ."). The horseman does not look back, but rides relentlessly toward the grandson, who is experiencing the vision of man's compromised nature. The closing is a masterpiece of understatement: "The world is real. It is there."

A companion piece of "Gold Glade" is "Dark Woods," in which the young man, perhaps now somewhat older and sadder, realizes he cannot recapture what has been lost. In the first poem of this subgroup, he stands in a dark field at night looking at the woods he played in as a child. He fancies that the field is full of other people—a hallucination rather like Hawthorne's Young Goodman Brown feeling himself surrounded by the "good" people of Salem at the Devil's Sabbat.

The other poems in this sequence explore further evidence for the irrational evil and suffering in the adult world. "School Lesson Based on Word of Tragic Death of Entire Gillum Family" gives a child's view of one of those irrational eruptions of violence in unlikely places —in this case, a decent but impoverished father who stabbed his five children, his wife, and himself with an ice pick. "Summer Storm (Circa 1916) and God's Grace" reveals that nature can be as irrationally dangerous as man. Men are helpless and stoical before natural destruction. That

poem and "Dark Night of the Soul" include childhood
memories that Warren used in his short story, "Blackberry Winter." In spite of its images of violence and despair,
however, the sequence leads to a lullaby for his sleeping
infant son: an invocation to "dream the world anew" to
"dream perfection," to "dream grace," to "dream
Reality."

Promises also contains a macabre inferno touched
with considerable folk-humor, called "Ballad of a Sweet
Dream of Peace." The persons who haunt this ghostly
limbo seem to be here because they have not yet attained
self-knowledge. When they do they are eaten by certain
supernatural pigs, a curious kind of eucharistic ritual to
illustrate that we are "all one Flesh."

The first strange sight that puzzles this visitor is an
elegant bureau all alone in the woods. The guide explains
that the bureau is there for the old lady who comes each
night to polish it. The old lady is the persona's grandmother.

> *Oh, what brings her out in the dark and night?*
> She has mislaid something, just what she can't say,
> But something to do with the bureau, all right.
> *Then, why, in God's name, does she polish so much,*
> *and not look in a drawer right away?*

Grandma does look in the top drawers, but hasn't got
around to looking in the bottom, where a tattered old-fashioned doll from her childhood lies, "that poor self
she'd mislaid."

When the persona hears a horrible chomping in the
woods, the guide explains it comes from the hogs he
slopped "in the dear, dead days long past."

> *Any hogs that I slopped are long years dead,*
> *And eaten by somebody and evacuated,*
> *So it's simply absurd, what you said.*
> You fool, poor fool, all Time is a dream, and we're
>   all one Flesh, at last,

And the hogs know that, and that's why they wait,
Though tonight the old thing is a little bit late,
But they're mannered, these hogs, as they wait for her
    creaky old tread.
Polite, they will sit in a ring,
Till she finishes work, the poor old thing:
Then old bones get knocked down with a clatter to wake up
    the dead,
And it's simply absurd how loud she can scream with no
    shred of a tongue in her head.

Later the visitor asks who that blind baby is who is
crawling through the black woods. He is outraged when
told that it is the "earlier one that they thought would be
you, . . ." "*But look, in God's name, I am me!*" The speaker
labors under the delusion that the conscious ego is the
whole self. The set of poems closes with a rumor about
God's intervention: ". . . there's a rumor astir/That the
woods are sold, and the Purchaser/Soon comes. . . ." This
section of the poem is entitled "Rumor Unverified Stop
Can You Confirm Stop."

Tale of Time

Warren's next book of poetry was *You, Emperors, and Others,
Poems 1957–1960*, not as remarkable as *Promises*, but
containing the excellent "Mortmain" sequence about his
father, discussed earlier. The next book, *Tale of Time,
Poems 1950–1966*, contains a sequence about the death of
his mother, also including his memory of the death of his
Negro mammy. Warren loved his mother very deeply, yet
she has not inspired as much poetry as his father and
grandfather. Without really knowing the reason for this, I
would guess that there was less ambivalence in his feeling
for his mother. Poetry arises out of some kind of emotional
tension and, in Warren's case, at least, a guilty awareness
of human imperfection. His guilt feeling in connection

with his mother is of a simpler kind, the regret for not
having cherished the loved one according to her worth.
This is expressed in a unique way in "The Mad
Druggist," about a pharmacist who was sent to a mental
hospital in Hoptown because he was making a list of
"folks that wouldn't be missed"—"If when I fixed a
prescription I just happened to pour/Something in by way
of improvement." The mad druggist tells Warren's
mother she would never be on his list.

> In Hoptown he worked on his list, which now could have
> nothing to do
> With the schedule of deaths continuing relentlessly,
> To include, in the end, my mother, as well as that list-
> maker who
> Had the wit to see that she was too precious to die:
> A fact some in the street had not grasped—nor the
> attending physician, nor God, nor I.

Warren uses biblical subjects for the first time in
Tale of Time, two poems under the general title "Holy
Writ." The themes are not different, actually, from his
usual concerns, the inevitable fall of men into sin and folly.
The first shorter poem, "Elijah on Mount Carmel," treats
Ahab, who was shown the truth when God ignited the fire
on Elijah's altar, while the priests of Baal prayed in vain.
Yet Ahab fled to "the soft Phoenician belly and
commercial acuity/Of Jezebel: that darkness wherein
History creeps to die." Warren has in mind here, I
suspect, not just the folly of an individual in a remote age,
but the flight of contemporary society from virtue to the
lust for material comfort. Ahab succumbs to the seductions of Jezebel, praying "Dear God, dear God—oh,
please don't exist."

The speaker in the longer poem, "Saul of Gilboa," is
Samuel, who annoints the beautiful young Saul with the
mournful foreknowledge that Saul will fall from God's
grace. The poem expresses again the idea that past,
present, and future are interlocked, interrelated. Samuel

identifies himself with all three, likening himself to a thin membrane through which the past seeps and into which the future bleeds. He tells Saul he will dance in God's favor, but he does not reveal the darkness that will follow.

> Say he will dance, but I do not say
> That that dance is a dance into self-hood—and oh!
> Beautiful is ignorance kneeling—and do not
> Say how black, when the dance-breath goes out, will be
> The blackness, nor say how the young boy
> Before him will sit, and strike the harp
> Nor how he at him, because he is young
> And the brow smooth, will hurl
> The great spear, and the boy will, like smoke, sway,
> Slip from his presence, be gone, his foot
> Leaving no print among rocks.
>
> He himself will become a friend to darkness, be counseled
>   by wolves.

Incarnations

Space does not allow detailed treatment of the many fine poems that have been pouring from Warren's pen in the last decade or so. From *Incarnations: Poems 1966–1968* I will comment on one, "Myth on Mediterranean Beach: Aphrodite as Logos." Rhymed couplets alternate with single-line stanzas in a distinctive use of the myth that Aphrodite, Greek goddess of love and beauty, renewed her virginity each year by entering the sea from which she was born.

This modern Aphrodite is, as the poem suggests, a parody of that marvelous maiden in Botticelli's famous painting of the birth of Aphrodite. This version, ironically associated with Logos (that is, the word, presumably, like Christ, of God's truth), is a humpbacked old woman with sagging belly and breasts, clad in a bikini. With her "contempt for all delusion," she makes the casual lovers strewn along the beach distinctly uncomfortable. Yet, her reenactment of the ritual rebirth through immersion in and reemergence from the sea is not entirely a mockery, though it may be so interpreted by many readers. The knowledge the observers gain from watching the ritual is obviously quite grim, but God's truth about the body is hardly encouraging. The old woman is as ugly and as old as she was before, in spite of the sacramental mode of her emergence, described as though she were a vision of loveliness.

> She moves toward us, abstract and slow,
> And watching, we feel the slow knowledge grow—
>
> How from the breasts the sea recedes.
>
> How the great-gashed navel's cup
> Pours forth the ichor that had filled it up.
>
> How the wavelets sink to seek, and seek
>
> Then languishing sink to lave the knees,
> And lower, to kiss the feet, as these
>
> Find the firm ground where they must go.
>
> The last foam crisps about the feet.
> She shivers, smiles. She stands complete
>
> In Botticellian parody.

As a revealer of the truth, which might be variously interpreted that physical love and beauty are woefully perishable or that there is something tawdry about casual sensuality, "She passes the lovers, one by one,/ And passing, draws their dreams away,/And leaves them naked to the day."

The tone of the poem is, I believe, easily oversimplified and may be rejected by some readers for its apparent mockery of ugliness and age. One must remember that old people, in Warren's poetry, often illustrate the world's pollution (like the old man with the wen in "Original Sin" or the beloved grandfather with the horrible faces of hanged men at his back), but they are not necessarily rejected for this quality. Victor Strandberg speaks of "the ironies of a fallen world undermining both" the Christian and Classical elements of the myth:

The logos of Saint John's Gospel has given way to its natural-istic successor, the "Polyphiloprogenitive" impulse to copulate spoken of in T. S. Eliot's "Mr. Eliot's Sunday Morning Service," which is the only primordial creative force visible in the living nature. . . . But Greek myth has also been undercut by the naturalistic awareness of our era, in particular the knowledge of time that renders the goddess of love a "Botticellian parody."[1]

What Strandberg does not make clear is the touch of ironic acceptance of the transformation in the rite. Aphrodite is herself in rapture, "For she treads the track the blessed know/To a shore far lonelier than this/Where waits her apotheosis." Perhaps Warren still has in mind granny's peculiar sanctification after she discovers her real identity—to be eaten by supernatural hogs in the universal eucharist of nature—"We're all one Flesh, . . ." If that is little comfort as a spiritual principle, it does promote some humility and pity for human limitations. Paul West has written in *American Writers* that "much of Warren's restlessness comes from his discovering that hard truths, even when swallowed repeatedly, do not soften."[2]

Audubon—A Vision

Warren's account of how he came to write his poem about the American naturalist and painter of native birds, Jean Jacques Audubon, illustrates how long a topic may lie fallow in the unconscious, finally to burst forth full-grown, like Athena from the head of Zeus. Warren says he started the poem in 1946–1947, when he was reading Audubon and other "sub-histories" of early nineteenth century, but it was all wrong and he cast it aside. "Then one day

[twenty years later], I remember I was helping my wife
make the bed, and one line from his old discarded poem I
had thrown away came . . . to mind, 'Was not the lost
dauphin,' . . . and suddenly out of that phrase burst the
poem . . . and a method for doing the whole thing just like
a vision."[3]

Warren never tried to find his old version of the
poem, but he does use that one line, which refers to the
rumor that Audubon was the lost son of Louis XVI and
Marie Antoinette. As a matter of fact, he was the son of a
merchant and slave dealer by his mistress, although he
was raised by his father's wife. This curious fact of history
is useful to Warren only in its relevance to the problem of
identity.

> Was not the lost dauphin, though handsome was only
> Base-born and not even able
> To make a decent living, was only
> Himself, Jean Jacques, and his passion—what
> Is man but his passion?

The second poem of *Audubon—A Vision,* "The Dream
He Never Knew the End of," combines realistic narrative
and concrete imagery with a mythic quality. Psychologically, it is the journey inward to meet the shadow-self or
the hag of the forest who, in folklore, preys upon lost
children. The persona, Audubon, has stopped at a hut in
the forest and asked for a night's lodging. The filthy old
woman in the cabin already has one night visitor, an
Indian who has damaged one eye. Both the Indian and
Audubon soon realize that this choice of shelter was
decidedly unwise. The woman's two hulking sons come in
and both guests are afraid to sleep in the presence of the
villainous family. Audubon identifies the situation with a
childhood nightmare.

> He has entered the tale, knows
> He has entered the dark hovel
> In the forest where trees have eyes, knows it is the tale

> They told him when he was a child, knows it
> Is the dream he had in childhood but never
> Knew the end of, only
> The scream.

Tension mounts steadily, the expectation of attack so imminent that he is paralyzed with a dreamlike lethargy.

> "Now, now!" the voice in his head cries out, but
> Everything seems far away, and small.

> He cannot think what guilt unmans him, or
> Why he should find the punishment so precious.

> It is too late. Oh, oh, the world!

> Tell me the name of the world.

But just at that moment armed men burst in and foil the attack. The would-be assassins are bound and gagged. Audubon thinks, "That now he will never know the dream's ending." In rough frontier justice, the three villains are hanged in the morning by the three strangers. Though the sons whine, the woman waiting for the rope neither weeps nor prays:

> "If'n it's God made folks, then who's to pray to."
> And then: "Or fer?" And bursts into laughing.

Before the hanging, however, Audubon suddenly perceives the woman's face as "beautiful as stone" and is sexually excited by her. Even in strangulation, the face with "Eyes aglare, jaws clenched, now glowing black with congestion/Like a plum," still seems beautiful to him, and he is filled with a desolate grief. He stands clutching his gold watch, which the woman had seen and coveted the night before, and thinks, "The magic of that object had been/In the secret order of the world, denied her who now hangs there."

It is easier to define what this does not mean than to state in nonpoetic language what it does mean. Audubon's spontaneous erection does not indicate that he is sadistically excited by the woman's pain nor does it suggest a sentimental softening of moral judgment of her character. (The black plum image may suggest the fatal fruit of the tree of knowlege.) It is more akin, perhaps, to a recognition of the attraction of opposites, especially order and disorder, or time and eternity. The bearer of the gold watch, that symbol of civilization's supposed mastery of time, is faced with a person who has lived entirely with disorder—outside of time, like the wild animals. Mythically, she is akin to the sea monster Tiamat, old Chaos, from whom the world is made after she is slain by Marduk, the mythic hero. Psychologically, she is the nonrational, instinctive, animalistic ground of being in the human subconscious that embarrasses the conscious ego. To live only in the logically ordered world or only in the instinctive, nonrational world is monstrous, since humans inhabit both worlds.

This particular definition of choices, between civilization's careful control of time and how it is spent and that other instinctive world of animals, is particularly pertinent to Audubon. He was one who never lost the lure of the timeless world and in fact neglected what "He had known he ought to be." Though he had a wife whom he apparently loved, he spent little time with her.

> Keep store, dandle babies, and at night nuzzle
> The hazelnut-shaped sweet tits of Lucy, and
> With the piratical mark-up of the frontier, get rich.
> But you did not, being of weak character.

> You saw, from the forest pond, already dark, the great trumpeter swan
> Rise, in clangor, and fight up the steep air where,
> At the height of last light, it glimmered, like white flame.

> The definition of love being, as we know, complex,
> We may say that he, after all, loved his wife.

> The letter, from campfire, keelboat, or slum room in New Orleans,

> Always ended, "God bless you, dear Lucy." After sunset,
> Alone, he played his flute in the forest.

Recognition came slow to Audubon. Daniel Webster offered him "a place," but Audubon declined—"I love indepenn [*sic*] and piece [*sic*] more than humbug and money." Eventually he won attention in Europe, whistling birdcalls in French salons, but wrote ". . . in my sleep I continually dream of birds." He returned at last to his home and wife—

> But the fiddle
> Soon lay on the shelf untouched, the mouthpiece
> Of the flute was dry, and his brushes.

Audubon "died in his bed, and/Night leaned, and now leans,/Off the Atlantic, and is on schedule." Warren seems to suggest that the time-ordered world has driven back the timeless world of nature, which Audubon yearned toward all his life and which inspired his art. "For everything there is a season./But there is the dream/Of a season past all seasons." These lines suggest that wilderness may be a paradigm for the lost innocence of a prelapsarian world. That may account for its fascination and for its power to inspire art.

In the last poem in the sequence, "Tell Me a Story," the speaker (now the poet) remembers listening, as a child in Kentucky, to the geese hooting northward. The poem implies, without saying so, that the feeling he had then must have been akin to that of Audubon. But his expression of that experience is found in literature. "In this century, and moment, of mania,/Tell me a story." "The name of the story will be Time,"—but you mustn't say so.

This poem has multiple levels of meaning. It is literally the story of a historical person whose life followed, at least roughly, the pattern Warren describes. But Audubon's romance with the American wilderness is also suggestive of Warren's lifelong love affair with nature. Warren's poetry, like Audubon's painting, requires the

nourishment of natural beauty. There are certain elements in this poem that suggest an even more personal
involvement with his shadow-self, if we may call it that
with the choice of imagery. Audubon's meeting the
hanged woman is very suggestive of Warren's boyhood
vision of his grandfather with hanged men at his back. I
am frankly somewhat puzzled by the presence of the
Indian in the story and the nature of his eye injury. With
little to go on except intuition, I suspect he is there partly
as an emblem of Warren's youth, when his own eye injury
led him to pursue poetry. Audubon's refusal of the
conventional role of storekeeping and baby tending brings
to mind the elder Warren's acceptance of just these roles
at the expense of his artistic aspirations. All this may
simply mean that a poet works from his own favorite store
of imagery. Warren's continued creativity, however, must
be partly due to the fact that old tensions stay alive
indefinitely in his psyche. As he expressed it, nothing is
ever lost. Quite aside from the historical narrative with its
personal echoes, the story concerns the change in
American attitudes, the fading of the half-mythical
character of the American frontier into the business-
oriented, practical, technological present. There is also, of
course, the psychological theme of the quest for identity,
which is universal experience and never far from Warren's
thought.

    Warren's later poetry reflects more and more a
comprehension of his life experience and an acceptance,
or at least a contemplation, of imminent death. One of the
neatest formulations of such self-awareness in modern
poetry is the verse from "Audubon" opening this chapter.

Or Else—Poems 1968–1974

Or Else contains many notable poems. "Chain Saw at
Dawn in Vermont in Time of Drouth" is as existential as

anything from the pen of Sartre or Camus and gripping in its compression. The irregular, occasionally spondaic rhythm reflects the violence implied in the diction.

> Dawn and, distant, the steel-snarl and lyric
> Of the chain saw in deep woods:
> I wake. Was it
> Trunk-scream, bough-rip and swish, then earth thud?
> No—only the saw's song, the saw
> Sings: *now*! Sings:
> *Now, now, now*, in the
> Lash and blood-lust of an eternal present, the present
> Murders the past, the nerve shrieks, . . .

Also existential in its vivid premonition of death is the excellent poem dedicated to I. A. Richards, "Time as Hypnosis." The poem concerns a snowfall when Warren was twelve years old, the first in two years in Kentucky and therefore wondrous to the boy, who wandered all day in the transformed landscape. The speaker observes the field mouse tracks which disappear abruptly in a wing flurry of snow, and intuits from them the suddenness and blankness of death.

> There was a great field that tilted
> Its whiteness up to the line where the slant, blue knife-edge
>   of sky
> Cut it off, I stood
> In the middle of that space. I looked back, saw
> My own tracks march at me. Mercilessly,
> They came at me and did not stop. Ahead,
> Was the blankness of white. Up it rose. Then the sky.

The child does not understand the significance of what he feels in this moment when existence faces the possibility of nonbeing. "All day, I had wandered in the glittering metaphor/For which I could find no referent."

"I Am Dreaming of a White Christmas: The Natural History of a Vision," in defiance of the banal title, is the antithesis of sentimental nostalgia—but it is the very texture of dream and the enigmatic gift of the past. The dreamer, warning himself with a premonition of dread at every turn, is nevertheless impelled to note each detail in dreadful succession. "*No, not that door—never*! But,/Entering, saw." The dust-covered room contains a Christmas tree, long past denuded of its needles; the skeletons of his father and mother in their accustomed chairs, staring out of their vacant eyeholes; three small chairs for himself, his brother, and his sister; and under the tree three Christmas packages. The dreamer realizes with a jolt that the holly is still fresh on the Christmas wrappings. He wonders which is his, but as he stretches out his hand, a voice out of the past admonishes him: "*No presents, son, till the little ones come*." The dream-self protests mentally that *he* is here, but the thought becomes a roar signaling a change of scene. He is standing in Times Square in New York City and the images have a bleakness suggestive of Eliot's "Wasteland."

> Old men come out from the hard-core movies.
> They wish they had waited till later.
> They stand on the pavement and stare up at the sky.
> Their drawers are drying stiff at the crotch, and
> The sky dies wide. The sky
> Is far above the first hysteria of neon.
>
> Soon they will want to go and get something to eat.
>
> Meanwhile, down the big sluice of Broadway,
> The steel logs jerk and plunge
> Until caught in the rip, snarl, and eddy here before my
>   face.

The wretched sense of pollution dissipates, however, when the dreamer imagines himself into another setting, the Nez Perce Pass, high in the Western mountains, where snow is falling. In the final stanza the conscious mind is trying to discover the logic of this succession of images. He decides "This/Is the process whereby pain of the past in its pastness/May be converted into the future tense/Of joy." Seldom has a poet captured so authentically the symbolic imagery of dream, its sense of horror and inevitability, and its mystery.

Can I See Arcturus from Where I Stand (Poems 1975)

"Season Opens on Wild Boar in Chianti" is remarkable for its rhythm and its sense of myth and autumnal ritual.

> They are hunting the boar in the vineyards.
> They halloo and hunt in the pine-glen,
> Their voices in distance are music.

The old boar, gorged on grapes and oak mast, seems almost a pagan god whose role is to try men's courage, "Each wondering who will be able/To choose his own ground when the adversary/Encounters him, red eye to red eye." But the boar dies, even as the old God of the Waning Year must always die in the autumn.

> The delicate, razor-sharp feet, not
> Now dancing, now dancing, point starward.
> They are lashed to a pole swung from shoulders
> So the great head swings weighty and thoughtful
> While eyes blank in wisdom stare hard
> At the foot-gravel grinding slow forward.

After the procession passes, ". . . we bolt up our doors, thus redeeming,/From darkness, our ignorant dreaming." One is reminded of the perceptive speech by Jefferson in *Brother to Dragons* avowing that all slain monsters and dragons are innocent. All heroes, whether Hercules, David with his sling, or Jack of the beanstalk, are playing in "the old charade where man dreams man can put down/The objectified bad and then feel good." "While in the deep/Hovel of the heart the Thing lies/That will never unkennel himself to the contemptible steel."

The best narrative, philosophic poem of *Can I See Arcturus from Where I Stand* is entitled "Old Nigger on One-

Mule Cart Encountered Late at Night When Driving Home from Party in the Back Country." Like Audubon's encounter with the wretched woman of the forest, this seems undeniably a confrontation with the shadow-self. The half-drunken reveler is careening down dark back roads.

> At the sharp right turn,
> Hedge-blind, which you take too fast,
> There it is: death-trap.
>
> On the fool nigger, ass-hole wrong side of
> The road, naturally: And the mule-head
> Thrusts at us, and ablaze in our headlights,
> Outstaring from primal bone-blankness and the arrogant
> Stupidity of skull snatched there
> From darkness and saurian stew of pre-Time,
> For an instant—the eyes. The eyes,
>
> They blaze from the incandescent magma
> Of mule-brain. Thus mule-eyes. Then
> Man-eyes, not blazing, white-bulging
> In black face, in black night, and man-mouth
> Wide open, the shape of an O, for the scream
> That does not come. . . .

The Negro's face is framed in a huge pile of junk he is hauling in his mule cart, a fact that is metaphorically convenient for the speaker's foreseeing of his own death. He imagines the old Negro's arrival home with his load of junk, his unworried entrance into his dark shack.

> And so I say:
> Brother, Rebuker, my Philosopher past all
> Casuistry, will you be with me when
> I arrive and leave my own cart of junk
> Unfended from the storm of starlight and
> The howl, like wind, of the world's monstrous blessed-
>   ness,
> To enter, by a bare field, shack unlit?
> Entering into that darkness to fumble
> My way to a place to lie down, . . .

In "A Way to Love God," also dated 1975, old crimes fade in memory, yet persist as a foreboding background to consciousness, and the sense of history is forever pregnant with new crimes about to be born, like Yeats's monster slouching toward Bethlehem. The persona speaks of mountains that moan in their sleep. In the daytime, "They remember nothing, and go about their lawful occasions/Of not going anywhere except in slow disintegration./So moan." The speaker calls this "the perfected pain of conscience," "forgetting the crime," a theme we remember from *All the King's Men*, where Judge Irwin is undone by the crime he did not remember.

> I do not recall what had burdened my tongue, but urge you
> To think on the slug's white belly, how sick-slick and soft,
> On the hairiness of stars, silver, silver, while the silence
> Blows like wind by, and on the sea's virgin bosom unveiled
> To give suck to the wavering serpent of the moon; and
> In the distance, in *plaza, piazza, place, platz*, and square,
> Boot heels, like history being born, on cobbles bang.

The speaker remembers the sheep huddling together at midnight on the mountainside, mute and unquestioning in their acceptance of destiny. The scholar, he who seeks knowledge, seems little better off.

> I watched the sheep huddling. Their eyes
> Stared into nothingness. In that mist-diffused light their
>   eyes
> Were stupid and round like the eyes of fat fish in muddy
>   water,
> Or of a scholar who has lost faith in his calling.

This sudden intrusion of the scholar into the rather dreamlike meditation is startlingly bleak, suggesting a sadly modern Job, perhaps, one who has had no direct revelations for all his questioning. God is silent and so is God's universe, in spite of all these hints and whispers that baffle interpretation.

Another recent poem that seems especially moving

and expressive of Warren's time of life, his patience and humility in the face of human limitation is "Trying to Tell You Something." The controlling image here is an ancient oak, split of its own weight, which has been braced with hoops and cables. It is a complex symbol suggesting, perhaps, all kinds of human contradictions that Warren has explored in both poetry and fiction—guilt and innocence, body and soul, past and present, illusion and reality. In one sense, of course, the mighty oak is a traditional symbol of strength and individuality, but here it is maimed and held together by artificial means. Its conventional significance is ineradicably changed, therefore, or perhaps even rendered absurd. It could suggest either the dissociated individual or the traditional culture itself on which poetry depends, which lives on as an anachronism in a scientific, technological world.

None of these suggestions is explicit in the poem, however—only the powerful image, the oak, "Immense, older than Jamestown or God, splitting/With its own weight at the great inverted/Crotch, air-spread and ice-hung, ringed with iron . . ." On a December night when the temperature falls below zero, the metal contracts with rhythmic throb and the cables sing in the wind. "In a thin-honed and disinfectant purity, like/A dentist's drill, sing. They sing/Of truth, and its beauty." The careful pairing of this truth/beauty with the image of the dentist's drill clearly proscribes any tendency to associate truth and beauty with joy.

> The oak
> Wants to declare this to you, so that you
>
> Will not be unprepared when, some December night,
> You stand on a hill, in a world of whiteness, and
> Stare into the crackling absoluteness of the sky. The oak
> Wants to tell you because, at that moment,
>
> In your own head, the cables will sing
> With a thin-honed and disinfectant purity,

And no one can predict the consequences.

This poem illustrates how Warren can, when he so desires, suggest symbolic meanings without being didactic and never pretending to more wisdom than he actually has. The promised revelation here carries more than a hint of the confrontation with death. Warren has never claimed that the self-knowledge that each man seeks is going to "save" him, whatever that means. (Was King Lear "saved?") It may destroy him utterly. Reality is not necessarily benevolent, and Warren seems always to have had grave doubts whether Truth, with a capital T, might be more than anyone can bear. It might, therefore, be both appropriate and necessary that Truth can be known only after suffering and at the point of death. Yet, such is the persistence of the mind that inquires into reality that even the promise of dreadful knowlege is somehow a comfort.

The stricken oak sings, not in its natural state or even in its summer raiment of leaves (which hide the cables), but in winter barrenness at year's end—spread-eagled, so to speak, to the elements. Moreover, it is the bondage itself, the tension between its twinned halves, its painful duality, that brings forth the song in its severity and beauty. Warren does not offer any final meaning for this image, but the reader should recognize many applications. I suppose the most basic philosophical bind is simply that human aspiration is fatally bound and dependent upon a decaying body. Most people manage to hide this knowledge from themselves for as long as possible. Warren does not do so. His late poetry is as good as or better than ever because he dares to face the conditions of his life, which are analogous to the conditions of all our lives, with an ever fresh and powerful metaphor.

5

From Melodrama to Pastoral: Later Novels

Band of Angels (1955)

Warren's later novels have never equaled in quality *World Enough and Time* and *All the King's Men*, yet each is an engrossing study of alienation in its many forms. The term *angels*, which seems so inappropriate to the persons in this novel, may come from *angelism*, used by Jacques Maritain to indicate a flight from the real world into an abstract world of idea.[1] *Band of Angels* is a melodramatic story of the identity problems of Amantha Starr, raised by an indulgent father as a white woman and kept ignorant of the fact that her deceased mother was a slave. When her father dies unexpectedly and somewhat scandalously in the bed of his mistress, Manty is seized by her father's creditor and sold as a slave. A kindly, middle-aged man, Hamish Bond, buys her to save her from the worst humiliations of the slave market. He soon becomes both a surrogate father and a lover. He has been a slaver in the past, however, and has ambivalent feelings of guilt, compassion, and sometimes contempt for blacks. When the area is occupied by Northern troops during the Civil War, Hamish gives Manty her freedom papers and turns her out. She marries an idealistic young federal officer, Tobias Sears, and lives an uneasy married life, torn by conflicting loyalties to both Negroes and whites.

The issues of race and miscegenation serve mainly to

intensify the theme of combined love and hate. Manty's ambivalent feelings for her various protectors (father, master, fellow slave, husband) are reflected in the strained father-son relationship between Hamish Bond and Rau-Ru, his *k'la* (favorite slave), whom he rescued as a newborn babe in Africa and raised almost as a son. Rau-Ru, forced to flee for striking a white man who was trying to assault Amantha sexually, becomes the leader of runaway slaves who become guerilla fighters against the Southern white community.

Manty's husband is rebelling against a father in the East, who is equally devoted to idealistic rhetoric and social status. Judging from old man Sears's inflated diction, Warren is showing again, I believe, his contempt for Emerson, and, by extension, that regional irritation with all Northern ivory-tower moralists who know nothing of the complexities of Southern experience.

The final episode of the book, which presumably provides some kind of object lesson of forgiveness and reconciliation, is an implausible reunion between a successful black man from Chicago and his filthy, garbage-man father who had deserted him as a child. The episode is an obvious and unconvincing contrivance to achieve some psychic change in Tobias, who braves social contempt by helping the successful son to scrub the accumulated stench from his old father and buy new clothes for him in the best stores. Presumably, Tobias's insight may allow Amantha to shuffle off the spiritual chains that still cling to her. We are so used to "poor little Manty's" habitual self-pity, however, that we doubt her ability to declare herself free of the past.

No one in this book is very likable. If the odious theology student Seth Parton (Amantha's first "crush") and his friend Tobias are absurd in their inflated devotion to religious and humanistic ideas, respectively, Amantha is annoying in her total lack of any social commitments. Her crises are largely in the bedroom, motivated by her need for love and protection from the cruel world. She manages to betray Hamish Bond, Tobias, and Rau-Ru, at one time or another; even when a child, she unintentionally causes a faithful slave of her father's to be sold down the river.

We have noted in Warren's novels that the tragic hero is often a passive character who is stimulated into action by a more dynamic person (Mr. Munn by Christian, Jeremiah by Wilkie Barron, Jack Burden by Willie Stark). Amantha Starr, however, is a consistently passive person, who brings unhappiness to men without even trying. In one of the most perceptive reviews of *Band of Angels*, Leslie Fiedler, who called Amantha "a reasonably good woman, among Warren's gallery of bitches," points out the curious reversal of Warren's typical plot:

No longer are we confronted with an impulsive righter of wrongs, driven to compound evil in his fury at its presence in himself and the world, but rather with a passive sufferer, who in the immobility of her self-pity permits man after man to make of her an occasion for self-destruction.[2]

Both contemporary blacks and feminists may object to the view of black Africa offered by Hamish Bond's description of his exploits as slaver. Not only are the Africans presented as unbelievably savage, but the cruelest are certain Amazon women warriors who go on raids to provide Hamish with human merchandise. The women's fiendish bloodlust almost defeats the purpose of acquiring unmutilated live bodies for export. Is this intended as a stereotyped justification of slavery as an improvement over life in the jungle? Perhaps the horror of this scene is intended to counterbalance some of the scenes of racial violence that occur in the aftermath of the Civil War at home—a universalizing of the principle of man's inhumanity to man. But why the stress on diabolical females? Is Warren showing that women, whether passive like Manty or aggressive like the jungle Amazons, are man's downfall?

Apparently a woman is also responsible for Hamish Bond's original decision to become a slaver. He was presumably responding to his dominating mother's pretensions to aristocracy, which she equates with having many slaves. Such blanket condemnation of women seems to exceed the normal requirements of fiction and reveal, instead, a deep-seated resentment on the author's part. Warren would not be the first writer to "get rid of his sickness in books," as D. H. Lawrence once put it.

In any case, the African episode, whatever its distortions, is a return to nature, like Jeremiah's flight to the wilderness—the horror of deserting ideas althogether and sinking into the amorality of unrestrained instinct. There are some parallels to Conrad's *Heart of Darkness*, but Conrad showed the natives in a more sympathetic light than Warren does. Conrad, indeed, shows that the presumed cannibals in the river boat crew had more restraint and humanity than the irresponsible white men who were raping Africa. Conrad shows a woman at the heart of darkness, too, as a symbol of wild nature, namely, Kurtz's mistress. As a parting image, she has a certain dignity and grandeur, however, as Marlowe looks back at her—not quite the same as Warren's fiendish warrior women. Perhaps, however, we are simply observing the convention that nature is female, just as, in Warren's next novel, the cave image is traditionally female.

The Cave (1959)

The Cave examines the impact on a small Tennessee town of the entrapment underground of young Jasper Harrick,[3] eldest son of a once powerful blacksmith, Jack Harrick. The old man, now confined to a wheelchair with terminal cancer, represents a legendary breed: the brawling, hard-drinking, hard-loving mountain man with the engaging grin, who becomes reluctantly civilized by a sedate young gradeschool teacher who knows what she wants. When Celia, that teacher, first sees Jack Harrick, he is riding in the back of a pickup truck holding up triumphantly the still bloody hide and head of a bear he had killed. Jack's early companion in mayhem, MacCarland Sumpter, had long since foregone his wild ways by getting religion. He had become a Bible-thumping Baptist preacher and obligingly married a young woman whom Jack had got pregnant. He was secretly happy, however, when Jack's baby aborted spontaneously. His wife had later died bearing MacCarland's son, Isaac, who is now a cynical, bored young man, well educated in everything except wisdom and compassion.

It is really Isaac who is responsible for the gross exploitation of the cave tragedy, building it up into a media event. He believes it is his chance to launch a career in journalism. He and Jasper had found the cave together on Jasper's land and had planned to make it a tourist attraction like Mammoth Cave or Carlsbad Caverns. When Jasper enters the cave and never returns, Isaac searches for him at his father's suggestion. The elder Sumpter hopes that the experience will save his son's soul. Instead, it provides Isaac with an infernal temptation. Believing Jasper to have fallen into a deep pit they had both seen in an inner chamber, Isaac creates a story of Jasper being still alive in a narrow passage, but pinned down by fallen rock. He sets willing volunteers to digging with the hope of reaching the cavern behind Jasper from the top of the hill, since Jasper's body presumably bars the entrance. This gives Isaac time to publicize the event and arrange with the local Greek restaurant keeper to feed and house the curious throng that pours into the town to watch the rescue. Isaac's father is busy exploiting the situation in God's behalf, preaching and saving souls before the mouth of the cave.

Isaac, after playing the hero for some time, sup-
posedly bringing food and other supplies to Jasper,
eventually announces that Jasper is dying and wants to
have the cave sealed up with his body in it. In the
excitement, Isaac's father slips into the cave alone, daring
to proceed farther than Isaac had and actually finding
Jasper's body, dead but still warm, in much the same
situation that Isaac had imagined. He realizes that his son
is responsible for Jasper's death by preventing further
exploration. To save his son from public exposure of his
fraud, he transports the telltale supplies Isaac had left into
the hazardous farther chamber, where Jasper lies.

The cave is a multifaceted symbol, most directly
related to Plato's well-known parable of the cave in *The
Republic*, quoted in the epigraph. Socrates says of the
inhabitants of the cave, "Like ourselves, . . . they see only
their own shadows, or the shadows of one another, which
the fire throws on the opposite wall of the cave."
Socrates's companion questions their responsibility for
their own ignorance, which is also important in the novel,
"True, he said; how could they see anything but the
shadows if they were never allowed to move their heads?"
The entrapped throng in the novel, of course, is the crowd
of spectators that surround the cave as well as the family
and friends of Jasper, and the fire that reveals the
ludicrous and misleading shadows is suggested ironically
by the artificial light of television cameramen. Of course,
there are older shadows out of the past that have
influenced present action, particularly the legend of Jack
Harrick, which has become a burden to his sons, his wife,
his best friend, and Jack himself.

Most of the characters believe that they are not truly
responsible for what happens, or they compartmentalize
their actions so effectively that the right hand never knows
what the left hand does. The Greek restaurant owner,
Nick Papadoupalous, is almost as oblivious as a sleep-
walker as he carries on an adulterous affair with a waitress

while he fantasizes about Jean Harlow. MacCarland
Sumpter tries to hide from himself the meaning of his joy
when his wife aborted Jack's baby. Isaac does not initially
plan to deceive the world—it just happens. This lie just
slips out when he first comes out of the cave and the eyes of
the multitude are upon him. Later as he sits meditating in
the cave, he is possessed by his shadow-self.

> He seemed on the verge of the unveiling of truth. He felt a power
> grow in him. But it did not feel like his own power. It was as
> though forces beyond him were filling him, possessing him. It
> was like destiny. . . . He was nothing, merely the guiltless
> instrument of a power, but that power, which was not himself,
> somehow conformed to his will, so that his will was, guiltlessly,
> achieved and he was filled with the exultation of power.

Isaac never faces and recognizes his own monstrously
self-centered nature. He despises his father, harassing him
for naming him Isaac. He suggests that his pious father,
like Father Abraham in the Bible, is willing to sacrifice
him to God. He also resents that his Jewish name was
responsible for his unusual social success in college with
the wealthy "Goldie" Goldstein, then his mistress, now
snearingly termed "the Jew girl."

The two fathers, MacCarland and Jack, and even the
pathetic Nick do ultimately face the realities of their own
situations and attain some reconciliation with the past.
Sumpter craves punishment for his sins and confesses to
his old friend (and hitherto unacknowledged rival) that
not only was he glad in the past that his wife aborted
Jack's child, but he had the same evil joy when he knew
that Jasper, too, was dead. He wants Jack to spit upon
him, but Jack understands and forgives. Jack confesses
that he himself wanted his son to die. His motivation is
more obscure, but apparently it stems from Jasper's
reputation as mirroring the "old Jack" of legend. Jasper,
like his father, was known, or rather presumed, to be a
hell-raiser. Jasper won a medal for bravery in the Korean

War, just as Jack did in World War II. The old man has
been wondering whether he was truly individual or simply
like every other man. Jasper's death somehow gave him
back his unique self. (One cannot help remembering the
shadow of Warren's sense of guilt about living his father's
dream.) Jack seems to recognize, also, the justice of his
wife's charge that Jasper was trying to escape the Harrick
legend.

The cave image not only carries the Platonic
implications of illusion, but also other traditional symbolic
overtones, such as womb and tomb. At the end, Jack
becomes reconciled to his own imminent death and
conceives of it as reunion with the son he can now love.
Finally, the cave is a symbol of the female, for this is also a
novel about fornication, in all its variations, its basis in
brute animal instincts and its occasional elevation into the
rites of love. Although the heedless young Jack once
deserted a pregnant woman, Jack's younger son, Monty,
will marry the girl he has impregnated. Both Jack himself
and his wife and son have emerged from the shadow of the
Jack Harrick legend, with its implications of violence and
uncommitted sexuality.

Perhaps the broadest meaning of the cave, enclosing
all these associations with sex, death, and Platonic
shadows, is a symbolic representation of the unconscious,
from which arises human motivation. In this sense,
everyone in the novel, even the preacher, is rooted in the
cave, so often at variance with conscious aims and ideals.
What the young schoolteacher saw in the young Jack
Harrick with his infectious grin and the bear head held
aloft in triumph is the personified libido. She was as surely
drawn to that animal strength as the crowds are drawn to
the cave edge to gaze in fascination at the black hole
holding its human captive in thrall.

The preacher still simmers in his repressed sexual
jealousy of Jack Harrick. Jack himself hangs onto the
illusory shadow of his former potency. His son Monty

simply blunders along doing. what comes naturally with little awareness of consequences. Perhaps, after all, in spite of its unpleasant air of exploitation, MacCarland preaching salvation at the cave mouth was closer to truth than we thought. The unconscious impulses must be recognized and somehow transformed or sanctified. Not all who enter the cave win rebirth through the spirit. Isaac may have been closer to the fountainhead in his romance with Goldie Goldstein, whom he later despised, than in the cave siphoning his feeble energies through a corrosive intellect.

Somewhere in the complex literary background that nourishes such a story, I sense the ghostly presence of Joseph Conrad. If *At Heaven's Gate* was inspired by the seventh circle of Dante's *Inferno*, then *The Cave* may be dimly beholden to *Heart of Darkness*. Unfortunately, it does not approach the power of that symbolic masterpiece. In *Heart of Darkness* the personal psychological element of unrestrained instinct is firmly held in place by a very concrete demonstration of social crimes. Thus, the jungle setting, the sociological situation, and the psychological implications all focus on the overpowering central symbol of the mysterious Self at the heart of the inner darkness. Warren attempts to build a somewhat comparable symbolic geography, perhaps, out of the sad vanities of young love, the miscarriages of friendship, and the inadequacies of parents. Since the novel seems quite frail to carry such a symbolic load, it may be wiser to look upon it as an interesting exploration of public and personal reaction to a media-created "disaster." Warren devoted two of his most recent poems ("Speleology" and "Cthonian Revelation: A Myth") to cave experiences, however, demonstrating his continued interest in their symbolic suggestiveness.

Wilderness: A Tale of the Civil War (1961)

Like *The Cave*, *Wilderness* is also an examination of the impact of illusion, this time on a young clubfooted

Bavarian Jew, who emigrates to America during the Civil War to fight for freedom. His father had fought for freedom and been imprisoned for it in Berlin. After his release he had returned to Bavaria to die. When his father's body is in the grave, young Adam Rosenzweig realizes that he has "lived only in the dream of his father's life, the father's manhood, the father's heroism." Now he must create a self of his own.

Adam endures a long and disillusioning odyssey to fulfill his dream, even though everything he experiences is contrary to his altruistic expectations. He is unsuccessful in concealing his deformity, even though he wears a specially formed boot and has practiced painfully to walk like other people. When he is refused enlistment among the mercenaries, he jumps ship in New York City. His first encounter is with a Negro hanged from a lamppost. The black's toes and fingers have been chopped off, an ironic reminder of Adam's clubfoot. He is caught up in a race riot; Northern whites are killing blacks out of frustration for being unwillingly conscripted to fight for freedom of slaves.

Adam finds something to ease his emotional shock at this reversal of expectations. He is saved from the rapacious mob by a black man; not until much later does Adam discover that self-interest rather than altruism motivated this act. Indeed, Adam persistently reinterprets human behavior whenever he can to keep alive his ideal of human brotherhood.

A wealthy New York relative, Aaron Blaustein, wants Adam to take the place of his son who died in the war. Adam repudiates this temptation to live a life of wealth and ease and refuses to accept money. Blaustein sadly arranges for Adam and the Negro who saved him, Mose Talbot, to go South as helpers to one of his itinerant sutlers, Jed Hawksworth, to sell to the Union troops.

Adam resists further temptation to falter in his idealistic quest when he helps a young mother on a lonely farm, whose husband is dying of battle wounds. Although both Mose and Jed make sly remarks about his opportunities with the woman, Adam, who is a thirty-year-old virgin, does not take advantage of the situation.

When they finally reach the Union army, Adam is disturbed by the cruelty toward black soldiers of one of the most decorated war heroes. But when he tries to teach Mose Talbot to read, he is secretly repelled by Talbot's academic limitations. In a confrontation between Mose and Jed Hawksworth, Jed suddenly rips Talbot's shorts to reveal a branded W (for "worthless") on Mose's thigh. This was the mark put on blacks who ran away from a battle. When Mose tries to explain to Adam how it was, Adam loses his temper and calls him a "black son-of-a-bitch," the very phrase Mose has warned Hawksworth never to use.

Mose kills Hawksworth that night and flees. Adam, who finds the body, buries it in the forest, hides the wagon Hawksworth drove, and takes off with the remaining wagon. He realizes, however, that he hides the deed, not to protect Mose, but because he fears he will be accused of the crime. Both his deformity and his Jewishness contribute to the feeling that no one would defend him. Moreover, Adam realizes that, in one sense, Jed died in Adam's place, since it was Adam's condescension that brought Mose to despair.

In a remote area, Adam meets another spiritually crippled soul and asks for guidance in fording the river that still separates him from the battle area, a desolate region known as the "wilderness." The man and his wife are living in a miserable hovel by the river. The man had been a pacifist minister but, ironically, had killed a man in resisting conscription because he was against killing. Now an embittered outlaw, he murders and steals from soldiers. Adam gives food from his wagon to the woman and listens sympathetically as she shows him their child's grave. The woman then gives him an unloaded gun and instructs Adam on how to prevent her husband from murdering him. Adam follows her directions, attains the

further shore, and comes to some kind of understanding
with his would-be murderer.

At the end of the story, a group of starving
Confederate soldiers assault him, tip over his wagon, kick
him soundly, and strip him of his precious boots. A few
Union soldiers appear and begin fighting with the
Confederates. Adam, in considerable pain, just watches at
first, but when two Confederates gang up on one bluecoat,
Adam seizes a rifle and shoots one of the Confederates, not
because he is "fighting for freedom" but because he
perceives unfairness in this concrete, particular instance.
The rest of the soldiers dash off, leaving Adam to
contemplate his achievement of having at last killed a man
in battle.

Since one of the Confederate soldiers made off with
his special boot, Adam must appropriate the common
boots of the man he killed. The desolate thought strikes
him that he killed the man "because his foot was not like
mine," suggesting that his whole idealistic project may
have been motivated by his resentment of those more
perfectly endowed than he. He notes, with some amusement, however, that his new boots are federal issue; the
Confederate had taken them from a dead Union soldier.
Thus, his new boots are community property, passed
repeatedly from the dead to the living.

He sees in the rubble of the overturned wagon the
little satchel that his uncle in Bavaria had sent with him.
Its contents have spilled out, but Adam soon spots the
three religious objects it had contained, the phylactery,
the talith (prayer shawl), and the siddur (prayer book).
He has never used them and does not do so now; but he
does kneel and repeat the Jewish prayer he had said at the
death of his father, which ends "Have mercy upon the
remnant of the flock of Thy hand, and say unto the
Destroying Angel, Stay thy hand." He rises in a new
humility, having given up his pretensions to the timeless
world of moral absolutes, and steps forth, as best he can in

his borrowed footware, in the real world of time and contingency.

As always, Warren has used numerous symbols in this novel. The deformed foot is the human flaw that prevents his ever performing the role of the hero he would like to be, although, ironically, some mythologies have suggested that lameness is a sign of the hero. It is a heritage from his father, just as the attempt to correct the flaw is a heritage from old Jacob in Bavaria, who had learned to be an excellent shoemaker although the smell of tanning leather had originally nauseated him. Old Jacob (like Warren's father) had learned to live with the limitations of his life. The satchel from his uncle also represents, of course, a part of his heritage, which he must accept as some kind of mixed blessing. In philosophical terms, his cultural background has given him contradictory commands: to suffer with patience, awaiting God's justice (as his uncle in Bavaria would have him do) or to fight for human justice (as his father had done).

Cave symbolism appears, also, in the early episode of the race riot. After trying unsuccessfully to stop a mob from slashing a black man with knives, Adam retreats into a dark cellar where many blacks are hiding. The crowd finds a hose and starts filling the small basement with water. One after another, the blacks panic and run out into the waiting arms of the murderous crowd. Adam feels his way to a high shelf and Mose Talbot helps him to climb up on it. As Mose explains later, there was only room for two; Mose helped him so that the other persons hiding would not hear Adam struggling and rush to find a place there. The water-filled cellar has implications of the womb, from which a new relationship is born (between Adam and Mose); Plato's cave, where Adam misreads a selfish act as an altruistic one; and the unconscious, where Adam meets his shadow-self. Later, Mose's pathetic struggle to master a written language he cannot understand mirrors Adam's extreme alienation in a world that does not share his ideas. Adam cannot "read" the world, for instance, when confronted with the animosity of an anonymous man on the road.

Name symbolism is prominent. Although Adam is proud of his name, which means "man," Mose gives him a less dignified one, Slew, for "slew-foot" emphasizing the very flaw Adam has sought to hide. Mose, on the other hand, refuses to be called by his first name, with its Hebraic overtones, but insists that Adam call him Talbot, which is an assumed name, to hide his identity as a "worthless" soldier. Ironically, however, Mose does act ultimately as one who reveals truth to the protagonist— truth about the real world, not, like the biblical Moses, the timeless world of moral absolutes.

In some ways, this novel is quite different from the preceding ones, conspicuously in the absence of complication. It has none of those little subsidiary narratives about supporting characters that provide depth and contrast to the main plot. Some readers may consider what Charles Bohner calls an "uncluttered narrative"[4] an improvement. But the characters seem to me to lack development. Even Adam has little substance, remaining almost a disembodied idea. In one sense, this is appropriate, since he is one who lives in ideas and finds it very difficult to express them in concrete situations. (He is akin to, but not as competent as, that other Adam who assassinates Willie Stark.) If some novels, such as *World Enough and Time* and *Band of Angels*, seem almost too heavy with concrete detail, this one suffers from too little detail to support the intellectual, almost allegorical content.

Flood: A Romance of Our Time (1963)

Adam Rosenzweig's problem of finding good and evil inextricably mixed in the same individuals, including himself, also oppresses the protagonist of *Flood*. The problem that bothers Brad Tolliver, as a writer and a man, is more accurately, however, the illusive quality of reality. "What always worried you was to find something real in the middle of all the fakery," says Brad, as he contemplates the vulgarities of the Seven Dwarfs Motel. "It worried you, because if everything is fake, then nothing matters." Brad is neither as naïve nor as innocent as Adam, but neither is he supremely callous and cynical like Slim Sarrett. Moreover, while Slim made up a "colorful" barge-captain father to romanticize his past, Brad really was begotten by a crude, half-civilized ruffian from the swamps. Brad is a writer of some skill who has succumbed to the Hollywood goal of giving the public what it wants. He looks upon people simply as grist for his writing mill, converting even his own experience into some variation of soap opera.

As the story opens, Brad is bent on exploiting a situation that could result in a real nostalgia piece: his tiny hometown of Fiddlersburg, Tennessee, is going to be inundated by water because of the new dam being built by the Tennessee Valley Authority. The inhabitants will be relocated at government expense, but some have lived there all their lives. A poignant situation, indeed, for some, such as the beautiful blind girl, Leontine Purtle, who knows every inch of the town so well that she can move about like a sighted person.

Brad's boss in this project is a Hollywood producer, Yasha Jones, famous for his documentaries. Yasha, ironically, is concerned with the truth of human experience, not the fakery that Brad has learned to use. Brad is disconcerted to discover that Yasha chose him as writer, not because of his recent success in popular fiction, but because of the earlier, more authentic stories he wrote about Fiddlersburg as a college student. Thus, Yasha appeals to a kind of innocence that Brad has already trodden down. This is not because Yasha is naïve but because, unlike Brad, he has already made peace with himself. He can now look at the world with a fresh, disinterested eye, unencumbered by his own emotional needs. The novel approaches, therefore, not only the problem of defining the true self, but also that of defining truth in art. The aesthetic message is not entirely clear, although Yasha utters some quotable quotes on the subject. Yasha says, for instance, that "science is the right telling. And that art is the right not-telling." He wants "to give the impression of the mysterious inwardness of life, . . . not the obvious plottiness." Presumably, the novel itself is "not-telling" but dramatizes that "mysterious inwardness."

Most of the significant action of the novel is in the past; we learn it in bits and pieces as remembrance, or occasionally through dialogue with Yasha. (Yasha is remarkably like a psychologist who listens to everything without prejudice and says almost nothing.) The tortured memories include Brad's past affairs with women, whom he uses to support his lust and his ego. He suffers from a need to create a more dramatic personal story than his humble background can provide. Thus, he goes to fight in Spain, not through political conviction, but to acquire the romantic aura of the hero. His models are undoubtedly the protagonist of *For Whom the Bell Tolls*, and Hemingway himself, who created his own legend. Brad also wanted to impress his current love, the politically involved Lettice Poindexter.

What he remembers most reluctantly, however, happened right in Fiddlersburg: a heedless, drunken debauch, which resulted in his sister Maggie's being raped or seduced by a guest, which resulted in Maggie's husband Calvin shooting said guest, which resulted in Cal's being incarcerated in the penitentiary outside of town. The big ruckus also resulted in a spontaneous abortion of the child Brad had fathered on Lettice that wild night, and the painful parting between Lettice and Brad.

The dramatic crisis almost has a rerun when Cal hears that Maggie is taking long walks now with Yasha Jones. Cal breaks out of prison and confronts the new rival with apparent intent to kill, but Brad receives the bullets in trying to prevent this new homicide. The shocked Cal then regains his repressed skill as a medical doctor and saves Brad's life.

Despite the "plottiness" of these events, the novel reveals that the motivations behind the actions are always much more complex than they seem. There is an old, unresolved rivalry, for instance, between Calvin and Brad, who were college buddies. Not only is Brad largely responsible for the situation that led to his sister's rape, but he is also in some fashion responsible for Calvin's sense of inadequacy, which begets violence to prove his manhood. Indeed, the shooting of Brad seems almost the fulfillment of subconscious desire. There is that sense of destiny or fate working itself out that is often an element in Warren's novels.

Ironically, this new crime has a rather happy resolution for Yasha, Maggie, and even for Cal, but not for Brad, who seems a broken man. He has learned to live, however, with his "original sin": ". . . he had learned that you can learn to live with anything, and had, in the long months, come to a grim acceptance of that black beast with cold fur like hairy ice that drowsed in the deepset inner dark, or woke to snuffle about, or even, as now, might heave unexpectedly at him and breathe upon him."

Unlike many of Warren's other protagonists, Brad does not have very far to go to retreat into brute nature. Brad does so when he goes to drink with his degenerate childhood chum, Frog Eye, who lives in the swamp. He is, I suppose, something of a shadow figure to Brad, mirroring his more beastly attributes but not personally necessary to the central events of love and revenge. Frog Eye witnessed the violation of Maggie while pretending to be in a drunken sleep.

Brad sinks into nature in another sense when he seduces the blind girl, Leontine, and takes her, appropriately, to the tacky Seven Dwarfs Motel. He tries to imagine himself in some altruistic pose on this occasion, thinking he will marry her and thus help her through the traumatic relocation. His spurious dream receives a severe jolt of reality when he realizes that she is far from the virginal innocent he imagined. Indeed, she is an old hand, perhaps even a professional, in the sex business. She adds a subtle touch to the theme of illusion and the difficulty of self-knowledge. She says, "Being you is like being blind."

Although Brad never seems to win through to some clear redemption, he does know himself much better by the end of the novel. Moreover, his symbolic shedding of blood, which saved Cal, Maggie, and Yasha from further tragedy, has mitigated, perhaps, the burden of his guilt. Even this final climax of his Fiddlersburg experience (that is, being shot) is not what it seems. His action, which looked like conscious martyrdom for another human being, was little more than a reflex action, like Adam Rosenzweig's impulsive shooting of the Confederate soldier. Thus, he knows that it must join those other acts, such as his fighting in the Spanish civil war, that cannot or should not reflect any glory upon himself. Yet, he cannot rest in cynical nihilism either, for there is still always that element of the real in all the fakery. He recognizes the solidity of his sister Maggie, of Yasha, of Calvin, of his flamboyant former wife, Lettice, even of his long dead father, whom he had despised for both his brutality and his human weakness.

Meet Me in the Green Glen (1971)

> My love is of a birth as rare
> As 'tis for object strange and high:
> It was begotten by Despair
> Upon Impossibility.
>
> Andrew Marvell (quoted in the epigraph)

Meet Me in the Green Glen, which is not subtitled a romance, is nevertheless, a naturalistic version of Sleeping Beauty in which the princess, though awakened, does not live happily ever after and the prince is hanged for murder. It is also a novel about loneliness and what it makes people do.

The enchanted castle is a run-down, remote farmhouse in Tennessee, where a fortyish housewife in slatternly clothes lives alone except for a husband long paralyzed from a massive stroke. Sunderland Spottwood cannot move from the neck down or speak, but occasionally he utters an inhuman sound to attract attention. In spite of the fact that she never loved him even when he was "alive," Cassie Spottwood devotes her life to his care.

The handsome prince is a young Sicilian immigrant with an imperfect command of English, Angelo Passeto. He comes walking up the road in his inappropriate city clothes, like the wretched tramp in "Blackberry Winter." He has been in prison and is evading his probation officer and ill-defined threats from former companions. Cassie invites the stranger to stay and work around the place; Angelo accepts thinking that "they" will never find him here.

These two persons, so ill-suited to each other by age and cultural background, become lovers, but initially not because they know and care for one another. She spies upon him out of the sheer poverty of her emotional life, and he rapes her out of undefined rage and the will to dominate. From this beginning in raw bestiality, a strange tenderness develops between them, partly because of their learning a little about each other's pathetic past but mostly because of the need for romantic illusion. He buys her a red dress and high-heeled slippers and shows her how to do her hair becomingly, and she feels young and beautiful for the first time in her life. She does not seem to realize or care that he is falsifying their relationship by transforming her into a "scarlet woman." They dance in the barren kitchen to the sound of the phonograph. Only occasionally does the horrible, inhuman sound of the immobile husband interrupt their lovemaking.

In spite of Cassie's malleability, Angelo feels trapped and cultivates a romance with the nearest neighbor, a black girl more nearly his own age, who is the illegitimate daughter of Sunderland Spottwood by his Negro mistress. Cassie, though jealous, assures Angelo that he is free to come and go as he pleases, for she knows all too well the agony of human bondage. But Angelo, not understanding the racial situation in the tiny Southern community, tries to take his Negro girlfriend to town to the Negro dance hall. He is beaten and jailed for a short time.

Murray Guilfort, a well-to-do lawyer, who has been subsidizing Cassie under the pretense of handling Sunderland's investments, warns Cassie that Angelo is going to be picked up for parole violation if she doesn't send him away. Murray, having always taken joy in the downfall of his friend and rival, the once arrogant and dominating Sunderland, is suspicious and resentful of Angelo's place in the Spottwood household. Cassie gives Angelo her car and a little money she has saved, tells him to take the girl and flee. In her loneliness and jealousy, however, she murders Sunderland so that Angelo will be apprehended and returned.

Cassie's revenge works only too well. Angelo is caught and sentenced to hang. When Cassie hears the sentence, she leaps up and cries out, "No! No!—I did it, I did it—I killed him!" Angelo responds to her anguished outcry with the cry "Piccola mia—piccola mia!" In that moment, at least, love strikes through all illusions, and each acknowledges the reality of the other.

To Cassie's consternation, her confession and her later frantic efforts to save Angelo are fruitless. Angelo is doomed, whether anyone believes Cassie or not, for he is a member of a despised minority and has violated the mores of the community. He is resented as an Italian who made love to a Southern woman and as a white man who ignored the race taboos with the Negro girl—even though he did openly what Southern "gentlemen" did secretly. One is reminded of Camus's protagonist in *The Stranger*, who was convicted of murder, not so much because the community cared about the dead Arab, but because the accused had not wept at his mother's funeral. Like Sacco and Vanzetti, Angelo dies because he is who he is. And he dies partly because he expressed love and received it in that courtroom before the eyes of his judges, who in the darkness and loneliness of their own souls envied him. Both Cassie and Angelo are described as having shining faces at that moment. In mythic terms, they have come to life (like the sleeping beauty in the fairy tale) in the midst of the emotionally dead.

After Angelo's execution, Cassie loses her reason and ends up in an institution. Ultimately she forgets the uglier details of her past, and dwells happily in a remembered love. Murray Guilfort, having maintained the illusion of being in love with Cassie all those years, finally realizes that he has never really known her. In his loneliness, he commits suicide.

As I have noted elsewhere, Angelo Passeto has distinct similarities to Conrad's "natural man," Nostromo. Angelo is the man of action and feeling, with little propensity for philosophic thought. He has a disarming directness but gives little consideration to the consequences of his actions upon others. He is, in some ways, peculiarly innocent, like a hedonistic child. When Cassie first learns about his having been in prison and treats him with an almost motherly compassion, his initial resentment immediately dissolves into real tenderness. As that other unsophisticated lover, Othello, would put it, "I loved her that she did pity me." But his tragic flaw is an inability to build on the kernel of reality in his relationship with Cassie. The house continues to exist for him outside of time—a place of blind lust and his tawdrier daydreams.

In one sense, Angelo is the opposite extreme of Adam Rosenzweig. Adam underestimates the importance of empirical reality, while Angelo, by ignoring the ideal world, refuses to enter into his full humanity. Like so many men, he is an accomplished lover with only a rudimentary sense of the spiritual possibilities in love. Perhaps because his is the more recognizable pattern, I find Angelo more credible than Adam as a fictional character.

The paralyzed man is the central symbol of entrapment in the flesh. His body as dead weight seems to become the spirit of the house itself. When Angelo crawls under the house to fix the plumbing, he is tempted to lie there inert, sinking into the ground with the full weight of the house bearing down upon him. This death wish mirrors the living death of Sunderland, who welcomes the real death Cassie finally provides. And in arranging for Sunderland's release from a living death, Cassie accomplishes both Angelo's rebirth as a morally conscious human being and his physical death. Thus, Cassie plays the three roles of the mythic goddess—mother, siren, and slayer—without being any the less credible as simply a lonely woman responding to the bleak circumstances of her own fate.

In psychological terms, Sunderland is Angelo's double or shadow-self. As Sunderland once betrayed Cassie with his Negro mistress, so Angelo betrays her also, with Arleta, Sunderland's daughter. In both cases, the black women were fundamentally unwilling participants in the affairs. Arleta, too, is trapped by the flesh; after the death of Angelo, she becomes a dope addict. In the complex web of human relationships, Cassie is the only one who survives with some equanimity, and then only by withdrawing from the real world into a selective remembrance of the past.

Although this novel will never rank with *All the King's Men* and *World Enough and Time* or even with *Night Rider*, it has a freshness and originality that sets it apart from other late novels of more complex structure. What it says about love is poignant without being sentimental, and it avoids the kind of emotional quagmire that seems to bog down the protagonists of *Flood* and *A Place to Come To* in the neurotic guilts of a lifetime. Perhaps Cassie provides the real clue to mental health—selective forgetting.

6

The Place He's Come To

Some critics regard Warren's most recent novel, *A Place to Come To* (1977), as more autobiographical than others, but Warren himself denies that assumption. The protagonist, Jed Tewksbury, rises from undistinguished beginnings in a tiny Southern town to be a prominent scholar and university professor in Nashville and Chicago. The genesis of the novel rests in an observation that may apply in some way to Warren personally, although he expresses it as a generalization about other persons. Warren says that Southerners who have despised and fled from the South never seem to feel at home any place else. The "place-to-come-to" is, of course, one's spiritual home, but the person rooted in the South may believe that his literal home stifles his possibilities for growth.

When Warren was asked recently whether there was any connection between himself and his protagonists, he answered no. He went on to comment specifically on *A Place to Come To*:

Quite a few reviewers said my last novel was an autobiographical novel. Well, it certainly was not. I didn't leave the South because I hated it at all. I lost my job [laughs]. I was fired twice down there. And my mother didn't write English like that, and my father didn't get killed by a mule's kicking him either. He died at 86 of a cancer he didn't tell anybody he had—an iron man. I tell you, that book's not even in any kind of a strange, twisted way autobiographical. Except one thing I've noticed about many Southerners who've left the South—people I knew, my generation or just a little bit earlier, a little bit later. They felt some kind of awful degradation about being a Southerner. Some of those people came north—some of them made terrific successes in business or elsewhere.[1]

Warren goes on to describe one such person who, after showing pictures of his houses, boats, daughters as debutantes, etc., exclaimed "Jesus, I'm lonelier than God."

It is possible that Warren "doth protest too much" the complete lack of autobiographical reference in *A Place to Come To* in order to preserve privacy for himself and others. Or any use he makes of his personal experience may be so changed or displaced as to be unrecognizable. In the novel, for instance, the death of Agnes, the protagonist's first wife, involves a lifting of her hand at death, as though to hang on to something; the gesture is the same one attributed to the persona's father in the poem "Mortmain." Of course, even in the poem the event may be fictional but other elements in that poem are apparently autobiographical. Jed Tewksbury also feels guilty about Agnes's death; it is a kind of guilt different from Warren's feeling that he stole his father's life but certainly related to career success. Such details, like the curious eye injury of the Indian in "Audubon," may be talismans of the author, private symbols woven into the fabric of any work he puts his hand to.

In *A Place to Come To*, the stigma on home (Dugton, Alabama) is not so much an original judgment on the part of young Jed Tewksbury as it is absorbed from his embittered mother. As soon as Jed graduates from high school, his mother insists that he leave Dugton and never return.

Other characters in the novel echo the peculiar alienation of homelessness. Jed has a torrid, adulterous affair in Nashville with Rozelle Hardcastle Lawford, who also came from Dugton and plans never to return. Rozelle

seems to have a neurotic need for affection, stemming
perhaps from her orphaned childhood, controlled by an
ambitious, unloving aunt. Jed's first intellectual mentor,
Dr. Stahlmann, a brilliant German scholar in Chicago,
is also a homeless person. He celebrates gaining his
American citizenship while America is at war with his
homeland—but later shoots himself. Late in the novel
Jed's best friend is a transplanted Polish Jew, who fought
against both Russians and Germans in Poland.

Jed is uncomfortably aware of the difference between
his wretched hometown and the home of Agnes, his first
wife, in Ripley City, South Dakota. He recognizes that
Ripley City is intellectually narrow and conventional, yet
it is self-fulfilling and friendly in a way Dugton never was.
When Agnes dies of cancer, her parents offer Jed a place in
their town whenever he wants to "come home" and even a
cemetery plot beside Agnes, should he want to come home
in death.

In the course of an emotionally stormy life, Jed
ultimately becomes reconciled to Dugton, however, and
even plans to live in his old home after his retirement. He
also tries to reestablish a relationship with his divorced
second wife, the mother of his only son. Thus, the rather
mournful story of frustration and passion ends with at
least the possibility of spiritual healing and the coming
together of a nuclear family with some sense of continuity
between the generations.

Much of Jed's hatred for his hometown is colored by
his hatred for his father, whose ignominious death when
Jed was a child left him and his mother destitute. The
episode opens the novel in what is surely one of the most
arresting first paragraphs in contemporary novels. It has
two sentences, one very long and one very short, an
unbeatable combination for rhetorical emphasis.

I was the only boy, or girl either, in the public school of the town
of Dugton, Claxford County, Alabama, whose father had ever

got killed in the middle of the night standing up in front of his
wagon to piss on the hindquarters of one of a span of mules, and
being drunk, pitching forward on his head, still hanging on to his
dong, and hitting the pike in such a position and condition that
both the left front and left rear wheels of the wagon rolled, with
perfect precision over his unconscious neck, his having passed
out being, no doubt, the reason he took the fatal plunge in the
first place. Throughout, he was still holding on to his dong.

To the squeamish (if modern readers are ever squeamish),
the coarse humor of this opener may seem more clever
than worthy of a serious novel. But it does suggest a
certain absurdity in human fate, like Kafka's brilliant
opener in *Metamorphosis*, where the protagonist has turned
into a huge dung beetle. In this case, sex and death
combine to make man ridiculous. Jed's father was a
handsome, promiscuous, alcoholic failure, and, of course,
the manner of his death made him material for folk
humor. Jed's continual susceptibility to both sexual
temptation and self-loathing possibly stems from his
ambiguous envy and shame about his father, who claimed
to have "the biggest dong in Claxford County."

There is more than a touch of Oedipal rivalry in the
situation. Jed faces his father's death at an age when
Oedipal feelings would be appropriate, and his attitude is
reinforced by his mother's anger toward her wayward
husband. At college age, Jed, who was a loner from the
very beginning, finally becomes a social hit when he
parodies his father's death. Thus, he converts his father's
manner of dying from a humiliation into a triumph for
himself. The comic stunt also conveys an implication of
sexual prowess, as inheritor of the man with the "biggest
dong in Claxford County."

When Jed first returns home from college unexpectedly, his untimely arrival in the middle of the night
interrupts his mother's first night with a lover. Jed's
confusion and disorientation are so great that he flees into
the night, like some kind of Hamlet appalled at his

mother's betrayal. Jed always remains in communication with his mother, but he never returns until after she is dead. At one point, he has an isolated sexual experience with an older woman (surrogate mother?) after they both watch the mating of the woman's famous stallion with a mare.

The man who shares his mother's bed, Perk Simms, becomes her husband, and, ironically, their marriage is a long and tranquil one, in contrast to the tortured couplings, marriages, and divorces going on in Jed's "outside" world. In fact, Jed becomes reconciled to the memory of his father only after he meets Perk, after his mother's death. Perk reveals that his mother's dying request was that she be laid to rest beside Buck Tewksbury. This is sad for the gentle old man left behind, but it establishes the pattern of family solidarity that leads Jed to try to reestablish a home with his second wife.

I am tempted to suggest that Warren may be catering to the public obsession with explicit sex in this novel; it does seem unnecessarily loaded with one bedroom scene after another. One of the comments in a group of men in Dugton discussing Buck Tewksbury's death-grip on his "dong": "Wal, a man ain't got that to hold on to he ain't got nuthen worth holden on to." The novel amply demonstrates this bit of typically male folk wisdom. The initial sexual episode with Rozelle is so precisely described as to the exact position of legs, knees, and asses, as to be almost ridiculous. It is not pornographic or romantic, just technical. To give the author the benefit of the doubt, however, the intention may be to emphasize the mechanical nature of this activity. (Perhaps one should compare it with Kafka's precise description of the difficulty of keeping the bedcovers in place when one has changed into an insect.)

Rozelle is described as having one arm over her eyes as though she had no consciousness of what is happening to her body. The whole affair occurs outside the usual time-space realm—and seemingly without volition. This radical dissociation between mind and body prevents the affair from developing into a real commitment between man and woman. Although Rozelle claims to love only Jed, she will not leave her husband, who has wealth and social status.

Rozelle and Jed have one other factor in common besides their sexual compulsions and their hometown. Each carries an ambiguous guilt with regard to the death of a former spouse. Rozelle lost her first husband under suspicious circumstances in a boating accident. The husband happened to be much older (and richer) than Rozelle, and she just happened to be having an adulterous affair with her present husband at the time. Whether there was actually "foul play" in the accident is not entirely clear. One suspects that even Rozelle does not know for sure; things just happen in her presence. (Compare Isaac's unplanned lie and the Greek's almost somnabulistic adultery in *The Cave*, and Cassie's almost unconscious provocation of Angelo in *Meet Me in the Green Glen*.)

Jed's odd case of guilt is more unusual than hers, but like her convenient accident, it seems to happen without his conscious volition. His initial success as a scholar depends primarily upon the death of his first wife. During the agonies of Agnes's last days in the hospital, Jed sits dutifully by her side and holds her hand, but when he goes home each night he works compulsively on an article which will bring him fame as a medievalist. It is called "Dante and the Metaphysics of Death."

And so life was really unendurable, for I began to realize that, in the mystic texture of the universe, my success would have been impossible except for the protracted agony and lingering death of Agnes Andresen. It was as though the essay had been, in the deepest sense of the work, her death warrant.

I had, apparently, on some moonless midnight, on a

desolate heath where the rocky, white, reared-up outcroppings grinned skeletally in the dark, struck a bargain with the Prince of This World: her life for my success. And he, like the gentleman he is, had scrupulously fulfilled his contract.

This quote expresses almost exactly the same sentiment as the passage quoted in another chapter about Isaac's sense of being the instrument of a power that was external to himself and yet conformed to his will (*The Cave*). Both Jed and Rozelle are in need of redemption for having accepted a spouse's death as a blood sacrifice for their own advancement. The status of spiritual crime does not depend upon literal causality. Jed's sense of personal darkness is exacerbated by his recognition that, although he truly loved Agnes after her death, he would not have loved her had she lived.

Perhaps Jed's problem is that he cannot, through most of his life, bring together the spiritual and the physical manifestations of love. He learns gradually to recognize when others achieve this miracle, as do certain of his Nashville friends (not Rozelle) and ultimately his mother and Perk. Jed's Jewish friend, Stephan Mostowski, acts, I judge, as Warren's mouthpiece when he suggests that the ideal must be bound to the material world. Stephan says to Jed, "Our souls speak in understanding, for we know that love is the poetry of substance and that poetry is the language of value." Jed achieves this fusion of idea and material reality in his love for his son, which leads to his reconciliation with his parents and his personal past.

Though he is not physically present when his mother dies, he undergoes a symbolic reunion with his mother by acting as a surrogate son for an unknown dying woman. On a dark street in Chicago, he witnesses an attack by two young hoodlums on a tottering old woman. He tries to intervene and is stabbed by one of the assailants, whose agility reminds him strangely, as he loses consciousness, of his own son, Ephraim. The boy had snatched the

woman's purse and leaped onto the hood of the nearest car
"to stand beautifully balanced there with the purse—like
Medusa's head hanging from the hand of Cellini's Perseus
in Florence. . . ." Jed's peculiar reaction to the scene may
be equivalent to the Ancient Mariner's blessing of the
water snakes, thus breaking the curse of the slaughtered
Albatross.

I remember thinking how beautiful, how redemptive, all
seemed. It was as though I loved him. I thought how beautifully
he had moved, like Ephraim, like a hawk in sunset flight. I
thought how all the world was justified in that moment.

    By then, of course, my head had gone very groggy.

When Jed wakes up in the hospital, the nurses assume
that he is the son that the old immigrant woman, now
dying, calls for. In lieu of the absent son, Jed holds the old
woman's hand as she dies, and arranges for her funeral
afterward. Following as it does a prolonged effort to
reexamine his own past, this event acts as a symbolic
death and resurrection, releasing him from his cynical
alienation from common humanity. So humbled, he goes
back to Dugton where Perk Simms, the surrogate father
he has never met, awaits him in his mother's house.

    When Warren was asked recently which of his novels
are the best, he named *All the King's Men, World Enough and
Time,* and *A Place to Come To.*[2] I would certainly agree with
the first two choices, but of the third I am not so sure. It is,
however, a better novel than I thought at a first reading.

    I would personally have wished more elaboration of
the experience connected with being a professor and a
scholar. Considering Warren's long immersion in the
academic community, I should think he could impart a
greater sense of reality to that element. Jed Tewksbury
might almost as well be a businessman as a professor. His
inward life of guilt and sexuality seems to exclude as
irrelevant his professional career. When his work does
become an element in his emotional life, in the matter of

Agnes's death and its relationship to Jed's insight into Dante, the nature of that insight is never disclosed. I, for one, would like some elaboration on this interesting point. If Warren were not such a perceptive critic himself, I would suspect the author simply throws in this implication of connection between literature and life without knowing enough about it himself to lend it plausibility. But that, surely, is not the case. Literature, of course, is the "not-telling," as Yasha Jones of *Flood* would put it; the action should be sufficient unto the meaning.

In this instance, however, even though I could speculate about how watching someone die painfully might contribute to one's understanding of Dante, it would be sheer guesswork as to which of several ideas was the vital ingredient. Would Jed's masterpiece concern the relationship between creative imagination and the desire for immortality? Between literature and real life? Between love as abstract contemplation of a divine Beatrice as opposed to love of a mortal woman who loses more and more of her lovable attributes as death approaches? Is death what makes illusion absolutely necessary, and do we honor Dante for the sheer grandeur of his illusion—and because now we have no dream equal to the fact of death? I am not sure what the point is, so I cannot tell whether the action of the novel demonstrates it or not. Perhaps I expect Warren to be an expert swimmer in the dream sea of ideas, whereas, in this case he is just pointing vaguely at the sea from the barren shore.

This hinting at unexplored philosophical depths is part of a larger tendency on Warren's part to blur the usual distinctions between moral, aesthetic, philosophic, and psychological issues. Thus, personal identity problems override social and political ones in *All the King's Men*, *Band of Angels*, *Wilderness*, *Brother to Dragons*. One critic has protested that there is no moral issue at all in *Brother to Dragons*, because Lilburne Lewis is obviously psychotic.[3] I am not that confident myself of the distinctions between mental sickness and what used to be called sin, but I should not like to see the older term entirely disappear.

Since fiction reflects, presumably, the inwardness of human experience, a dialectical swinging between opposite interpretations has a certain validity. It is the business of a formal philosophy to be logically consistent in all its parts. I doubt, however, that anyone in his actual living achieves any such stasis. If anyone seems to have done so, then he has escaped the stream of time and experience as surely as Warren's characters escape time by descending into the instinctual underworld, the "blank cup of nature." In psychological terms, then, Warren's fictional world may be a "true" one, in spite of philosophical ambiguities. From "Empty White Blotch on Map of Universe: A Possible View" in *Being Here*:

> I have written whole books, with a stone-honed reed on the sand,
> Telling truth that should never be told, and what such truths mean.
> But who cared? For Truth must accept its reprimand
> When the tide comes in like Christ's blood, to wash all clean,
> Including the truth that Truth's only a shout, or clapped hand,
> At the steel-heeled stomp, steel-throated bark, or a lifted wand.

Warren is too phenomenological to pretend to a neatly consistent philosophy. His gift is poetic—the image represents meaning better than argument, though he often tries to interpret the image. Yet he realizes a contradiction, even as he tries to eliminate abstraction from the direct experience of a thing. In the poem "Unless" (*Now and Then*), for instance, although he equates truth with the snake's discarded skin, his perception of the "real" snake is itself abstracted to "energy" and idealized to the point of religious sentiment.

All will be in vain unless—unless what? Unless
You realize that what you think is Truth is only

A husk for something else. Which might,
Shall we say, be called energy, as good a word as any. As
    when

The rattlesnake, among desert rocks
And Freudian cactus tall in moonlight,

Scrapes off the old integument, and flows away,
Clean and lethal and gleaming like water over moon-bright
    sand,

Unhusked for its mission. Oh, *neo nata*! fanged, unforgiving,
We worship you. In the morning.

In the ferocity of daylight, the old skin
Will be translucent and abstract, like Truth . . .

The allusion to "Freudian cactus" suggests a touch of
ironic parody. Even though Freudian interpretations
have nothing to do with "real" cactus, it seems to be
humanly impossible to look upon nature without inter-
preting it in relation to one's self and one's cultural
background. Thus, the "real" snake becomes a principle,
perhaps a representative of the unconscious, the libido, as
opposed to the ego. One remembers the contradictory
views of the snake in *Brother to Dragons*. The realistic
perception of the snake as harmless and natural never
dispels the mythical perception as pagan god. Indeed, the
snake serves no purpose in that poem unless it is
interpreted mythically. A wholly naturalistic snake is
quite irrelevant to moral questions.

Modern rationality is a late-comer on the scene,
however, and generally ineffectual against the mythic
imagination. We cannot eliminate the mythical, although
we may continually struggle to modify its terms.
Intellectually, at least, we crave a myth that is equal to
reality. And a man defines himself through the myth he
has chosen. Warren's myth is always touched with irony,

because he recognizes that he can never see a thing for
itself alone.

Warren's three latest books, *Now and Then: Poems
1976–1978*, which won a Pulitzer Prize, *Being Here: Poetry
1977–1980*, and *Rumor Verified: Poems 1979–1980*, continue to
finger the texture of experience, the truths of the senses
that he has stored up from the past, and his constant
struggle for some larger truth that will contain them all.
From "Vision": "Can it be that the vision has, long back,
already come—/And you just didn't recognize it?" This
sense of puzzlement, of unfulfilled quest haunts the whole
body of poems. Yet there is a richness and variety of
imagery that reveals a poet of great skill, not at all
diminished in his eighth decade. There is, appropriately,
a greater awareness of death, especially in *Being Here*, for
Warren has at last caught up with his favorite poetic
season, the autumn.

Now and Then has two sections. The first, called
"Nostalgic," picks up some of the familiar themes of his
childhood and closes with two poems apparently associated with his halcyon days in Italy after his second
marriage. The longer section, called "Speculative," is
more contemporary and philosophic.

The early poems, though autobiographical, are
interesting also for their evocation of a typically American
kind of experience. The first celebrates his old companion
who became a baseball pitcher and an alcoholic. It
combines so well a sense of the virtue and the promise of
the American "hillbilly," as a homegrown Adonis (or
perhaps another Huckleberry Finn), with a painful
acknowledgment of what modern experience does to such
a person.

> . . . how K, through lane-dust or meadow,
> Seemed never to walk, but float
> With a singular joy and silence,
> In his cloud of bird dogs, like angels,
> With their eyes on his eyes like God,

And the sun on his uncut hair bright
As he passed through the ramshackle town and odd folks
    there
With pants on and vests and always soft gabble of money—
Polite in his smiling, but never much to say.

To pass through to what? No, not
To some wild white peak dreamed westward,
And each sunrise a promise to keep. No, only
The Big Leagues, not even a bird dog,
And girls that popped gum while they screwed.

"Amazing Grace in the Back Country" recalls the
old tent meetings of the traveling evangelist and the
persona's rejection (at twelve years of age) of the offered
grace and his sense of hardened sin:

> . . . I knew I was damned,
> Who was guilty of all short of murder,
> At least in my heart and no alibi there, and once
> I had walked down a dark street, lights out in houses,
> Uttering, "Lust—lust—lust,"
> Like an invocation, out loud—and the word
> So lovely, fresh-minted.

The experience has some echoes of the early episode in
World Enough and Time in which the protagonist, older than
the persona of the poem, succumbs to the hysteria of the
tent meeting but runs out and assaults the old woman of
the forest. In the poem, an old woman tries to induce the
boy to kneel and accept the proferred grace, but he runs
out to vomit in the woods.

Irony is central to the poem, not only the ironic
understanding of the boy's somewhat abstract perception
of sin, but also the seeming futility of the exercise for those
accepting the amazing grace who "tomorrow would rise
and do all the old things to do/Until that morning they
would not rise, not ever." Yet, the poetic voice is not
contemptuous of these old passions, not even as he implies
that they are somehow analogous to the enthusiasm for

that other archaic institution that appeared periodically
in an old tent on the same ground: the traveling carnival,
with its freaks and mangy animals and old whores
"ready to serve/Any late-lingerers, and leave/A new and
guaranteed brand of syphilis handy . . ."

In "Red-Tail Hawk and the Pyre of Youth" Warren
uses the shooting of the bird and its later burning as
ritual rites of passage. Like the shooting of the bullbats in
"What Was the Promise That Smiled from the Maples at
Evening," the shooting suggests the "original sin" that
brings the boy out of the prelapsarian world of childhood. But the symbolic overtones of the hawk are more
complicated than those in any of the former poems about
the falling of birds. The hawk seems to represent both the
wild Other that man confronts in nature and the wild
element of the self that achieves definition in the
encounter. The hawk's ferocity appears in the blank sky,
rather like the vision of hanged men behind the
grandfather in an earlier poem. In this case, however, the
boy is equal to the challenge and brings down the bird
with one "impossible" shot—one shot that "breaks the
circle," a supreme breaking out of symmetry. The act
suggests paradoxically both a union with nature and an
escape from it.

> Except for the center of
> That convex perfection, not yet
> A dot even, nameless, no colour, merely
> A shadowy vortex of silver. Then,
> In widening circles—oh, nearer!
> And suddenly I knew the name, and saw,
> As though seeing, coming toward me,
> Unforgiving, the hot blood of the air:
> Gold eyes, unforgiving, for they, like God, see all.
>
> There was no decision in the act,
> There was no choice in the act—the act impossible but
> Possible. I screamed, not knowing
> From what emotion, as at that insane range

> I pressed the cool, snubbed
> Trigger. Saw
> The circle
> Break.

But the act is not just indicative of the boy's assertion of selfhood. The hawk is connected in a subtle way with the persona's early enthusiasm for literature. He stuffs the hawk (one of Warren's childhood skills) and places it on his topmost bookshelf. This could suggest a transference of the energy concentrated in the hawk symbol to the obsession with poetry. A stuffed hawk is, ironically, like the outgrown skin of the snake—a symbol of truth, perhaps, but also a cenotaph for vital energy. But poems, too, are the residue or skeletons of the vital creative activity of the poet.

> Year after year, in my room, on the tallest of bookshelves,
> It was regal, perched on its bough-crotch to guard
> Blake and *Lycidas*, Augustine, Hardy and *Hamlet*,
> Baudelaire and Rimbaud, and I knew that the yellow eyes,
> Unsleeping, stared as I slept.

The persona returns at a later and sadder time, "When my mother was dead, father bankrupt, and whiskey/Hot in my throat. . . ."/The now shabby hawk has been thrown in a lumber room along with other trash, but the speaker remembers and imagines the eyes staring in vengeance. He finds the hawk with other emblems of his youthful enthusiasms and burns them.

> And all relevant items I found there: my first book of Milton,
> The *Hamlet*, the yellow, leaf-dropping Rimbaud, and a book
> Of poems friends and I had printed in college, not to
>   mention
> The collection of sexual Japanese prints—strange sex
> Of mechanical sexlessness. And so made a pyre for
> The hawk that, though gasoline-doused and wing-
>   dragging,
> Awaited, with what looked like pride,
> The match.

Since this poem is dedicated to Harold Bloom, it may have a more esoteric meaning, suggestive of the poet's self-assertion over his poetic precursors (the hawk perched above the bookshelf). According to Bloom (*The Anxiety of Influence*), there is, of necessity, a kind of Freudian family romance between the young poet and the older masters (poetic fathers) from whom he learns. In order to assert his originality, the poet must "kill the father" in some metaphorical way, that is, pretend that he created himself (exactly what Slim Sarrett was trying to do in *At Heaven's Gate*). In order to do this, the poet may misread or otherwise discredit the literary father in order to assert his own version of what the older poet has said. He corrects God, so to speak—a project fraught with a certain burden of guilt, perhaps. Bloom suggests that Satan is a good analogy to the strong poet, because the poet must prove himself the equal of his great predecessors. If this is so, then Warren's "Pyre of Youth" may be an ironic recognition of this necessary, but somewhat pathetic, pride in placing himself in a commanding position (as the hawk) over Milton, Blake, Hardy, Shakespeare, and others who first fired his poetic imagination. Presumably, Warren is now old enough and sure enough in his poetic performance not to need this psychic crutch.

Bloom's ideas may shed considerable light upon Warren's obsession with identity and with his repeated use of the Adam function of naming things. "What is the name of the World?" This question (literally almost meaningless) or variations of it appear in many contexts, wherever the persona has seen the world in some new and usually terrible way. According to Bloom, to name something is the true originality to which every poet aspires. If one names something for the first time, it becomes one's property. After quoting Freud on the personal nature of the family romance, wherein the incestuous desire for the mother is really a desire to be "the father of himself," to discount his debt to his father,

Bloom suggests how this impulse works in the relationships between poets.

> If this is to serve as model for the family romance between poets, it needs to be transformed, so as to place the emphasis less upon phallic fatherhood, and more upon *priority*, for the commodity in which poets deal, their authority, their property, turns upon priority. They own, they are, what they become first in naming. Indeed, they all follow the intuition of Valery, when he insisted that man fabricates by abstraction, a withdrawal that takes the made thing *out from* the cosmos and from time, so that it may be called one's own, a place where no trespass can be permitted. All quest-romances of the post-Enlightment, meaning all Romanticisms whatsoever, are quests to re-beget one's own self, to become one's own Great Original. We journey to abstract ourselves by fabrication. But where the fabric already has been woven, we journey to unravel. Alas—in art—the quest is more illusory even than it is in life. Identity recedes from us in our lives the more we pursue it, yet we are right not to be persuaded that it is unattainable. Geoffrey Hartman notes that in a poem the identity quest always is something of a deception, because the quest always works as a formal device. This is part of the maker's agony, part of why influence is so deep an anxiety for the strong poet and compels him to an otherwise unnecessary inclination or bias in his work. No one can bear to see his own inner struggle as being mere artifice, yet the poet, in writing his poem, is forced to see the assertion against influence as being a ritualized quest for identity. Can the seducer say to his Muse: "Madam, my deception is imposed upon me by the formal demands of my art?"[4]

This passage, perhaps more than any other I have encountered in criticism, suggests an explanation for Warren's persistence in questions of identity. I must admit that identity never seemed like that much of a problem to me—I have accused myself, at times, of feeble complacency in the face of such anguished soul-searching. Perhaps the oft quoted question "Who am I?" has more importance for those competing with giants for a place in the sun. The quest, if I understand Bloom correctly, is not so much a universal problem as it is a poetic declaration of independence. Nevertheless, this impulse to break away and the anxiety that rebellion always engenders in the sensitive soul have sufficient analogues in ordinary life to justify the poet's imposing his private agony upon us all. He is offering a more intensified version of our common desire for uniqueness and individuality.

To turn from these speculations to other "speculative"poems in *Now and Then*, many have a haunting, dreamlike quality, like the poem appropriately named "Dream of a Dream." The following stanza illustrates Warren's sophisticated command of sound devices: rhyme, rhythm, assonance, alliteration.

> Moonlight stumbles with bright heel
> In the stream, and the stones sing.
> What they sing is nothing, nothing,
> But the joy Time plies to feel
> In fraternal flux and glimmer
> With the stream that does not know
> Its destination and knows no
> Truth but its own moonlit shimmer,
> In any dream Time and water interflow,
> And bubbles of consciousness glimmer ghostly as they go.

Sometimes, the ironic voice emerges, coupled with a helpless admission of the limitations of knowledge. In "Not Quite Like a Top," the speaker meditates in mock seriousness on the scientific claim that the earth's axis sways and swings from the middle. He tries to feel the sway as he lies in bed with his head to the north—a futile project, of course, but it brings up other more personal matters that are equally undemonstrable. He admits to weeping sometimes because "I couldn't be sure something precious was true." And he wryly remembers his youthful arrogance in the face of theological questions.

> Once, in a Pullman berth (upper), I desperately prayed
>
> To God to exist so that I
> Might have the exalted horror of denying

ness, as Twain did. The poem becomes a meditation upon how original goodness can leak away.

> And that night in bed, like a dream but not one, I saw.
> Saw inside of Zack's ruin of a shack, and a coal-oil
> Lamp flickered, and Zack and his Mag, young now,
> Getting ready for bed, them maybe just married.
> Saw how she was trying to get off her gear and not show
> That foot. Yes, there in my head, I saw it, and saw
> How he took it, the foot. Leaned over and kissed it.
>
> And tears gone bright in her eyes.
>
> But all the years later I'd only see
> How he'd try not to see it. Then
> Blow out the lamp. And if summer,
> He'd stare up in darkness. If winter,
> And fire on the hearth, lie watching
> The shadows dance on the ceiling. And handle himself,
> To make himself grab her.

The speaker, now camping in the woods of Ontario, admits to dreaming a "real dream," not about Zack and Mag, but about the train that "Comes boiling over the hill, whistle crazy . . ." He is awakened by the loon "laughing his crazy fool head off." The train here suggests the engine of death, the persona identifying himself subconsciously with the old persons struggling on the fatal track. He rises to a glorious day, far from any railroad tracks or other blemishes on the face of nature and wonders if it can be the same world that he has known in its darker guises. The poem is a skillful weaving together of contradictory perceptions about the nature of the world and human physical and spiritual deformities. The last scene might almost be paradise regained, except for the awareness implied in the foreboding dream of the train.

In his "Afterthought," Warren points to two poems, "Empty White Blotch on Map of Universe: a Possible View," quoted earler, and "Ballad of Your Puzzlement," as ironic "backboard" for the other poems. Many of the

Him. But nothing
Came of that project. Nothing. Oh, nothing.

Is this theological rebellion a different version, perhaps, of the romantic quest for identity, or, in Bloom's terms, the poet's necessary repudiation of his precursors? If so, it views such sentiments from an ironic distance, fully conscious of the adolescent quality in these old passions. The sly inclusion of the word "upper" suggests that the minuscule elevation from the earthly plane is indicative of how lofty the thinking was. Blessed are those who can live long enough to laugh at themselves! It is the supreme triumph.

Which brings up another poem, "Last Laugh," one of the most interesting in this collection. What more appropriate subject than Mark Twain to illustrate the connection between a comic and a tragic view of human existence? This poem is based on the biographical story that the young Sam Clemens witnessed the autopsy performed on his father. "Peeped through the dining-room keyhole, to see, outspread/And naked, the father split open, lights, liver, and all/Spilling out from that sack of mysterious pain, and the head/Sawed through, where his Word, like God's, held its deepest den, . . ." Since Sam's father was a rather cold man (Sam called their relationship an "armed truce"), the boy's subsequent weeping was as much relief as grief. The poem suggests that the event was closely connected to Sam's subsequent contempt for religion and his gift for mockery. "God was dead, for a fact. He knew, in short, the best joke." But Sam's reductive humor not only made him a success as a writer and lecturer, it also hurt the woman he loved: "For Livy loved God, and he'd show her the joke, how they lied." Eventually, "He watched dying eyes stare up at a comfortless sky,/And was left alone with his joke, God dead, till he died."

I wonder whether the story of Sam's early traumatic

vision of his dead father, so indecently exposed ("It's not every night/You can see God butchered . . .") might have provided an analogue for the opening of *A Place to Come To*. Like this poem, the novel begins with a humiliating vision of the dead father, which is later converted by the son into a joke. This attitude, though useful in the son's career, helps to alienate him from common humanity, and Jed Tewksbury seems to be heading for a bitter iconoclasm comparable, perhaps, with that of Twain's last days. Perhaps Bloom would say that Warren "corrects" Twain by showing a possibility for redemption, thus avoiding the plunge into solipsism revealed in Twain's *Mysterious Stranger*.

Being Here is Warren's recapitulation of some of the events or ideas that seemed important in his life, presented more or less chronologically from a remembered picnic in that prelapsarian world of childhood to a kind of benediction, "Passers-by of Snowy Night," ". . . Alone,/I wish you well in your night/As I pass you in my own." Warren warns us, however, in the prose "Afterthought" that "this is an autobiography which represents a fusion of fiction and fact."

Thus, "Speleology," the poem that follows the nostalgic remembered picnic, may record a real experience of Warren's finding a cave, at age six, and his venturing into it a little bit deeper each year until age twelve. Or the cave may be a metaphor for the evolving consciousness of the mystery of the self and, from the viewpoint of age, the awareness of death. (I suppose a Freudian interpretation would switch that to an awareness of sex, but that is a less valid approach in this particular case.)

> Lulled as by song in a dream, knowing
> I dared not move in a darkness so absolute.
> I thought: *This is me*. Thought: *Me—who am I?* Felt
> Heart beating as though to a pulse of darkness and earth,
>   and thought
> How would it be to be here forever, my heart.

The persona admits to asking this question repeatedly in later years. It closes with a different, but related question that must occur to every older person who realizes that most of life is in the past—"And in darkness have even asked: 'Is this all? What is all?'"

The early section has an interesting narrative poem, "Recollection in Upper Ontario, from Long Before," which has the familiar theme of "Blackberry Winter," the young person getting a glimpse of the grim adult world. It also has a secondary theme, perhaps, concerning the way in which an isolated act can be expanded into a dramatic narrative. The characters of the recollection are "Old Zack, pore old white trash" and "Old Mag . . . face knobby, eyes bleared,/Mouth dribbling with snuff, skirts swinging/Above the old brogan she's fixed for her clubfoot. . . ." (One wonders, though it doesn't matter, if this woman provided the germ for the clubfooted Adam of *Wilderness*, or the other way around.) The two are stealing coal from the railroad and the persona is the accidental witness, a boy catching butterflies with a net nearby. The train is coming and Mag has caught her clubfoot in the tracks. Zack is trying to loosen the brogan; it seems to be loose, then Mag falls and is hit by the train. The boy flees, not sure whether he saw Zack push her before the train or try to pull her from danger. The mystery becomes more menacing when the drunken Zack later grabs the boy and says, "Yeah, you come spyen on me!/Down thar in the ditch, in them weeds. Well, you're wrong! . . ./I ne'er tetched her! She fell. Nigh got myself kilt/Count of her durn shoe!"

So far, the story is reminiscent of Tom Sawyer's relationship to Indian Joe, but here the speaker turns away from the "real" event to improvise a history that would account for the act of murder. In other words, he creates a story about Zack and Mag, instead of resolving the potential conflict between murderer and wit-

poems are concerned, as he himself states, with reviewing his life from the standpoint of age. I suspect that he has been afraid of seeming to be sentimental, and his explicit pointing at these two ironic poems is designed to protect him from such a suspicion. They also reinforce his statement that the autobiographical elements in the poems may be blends of fact and fiction, as though to say, "I may be baring my soul, but only I know what is authentically me." Or perhaps Warren wouldn't say that at all, but rather, "Even I do not know what is true about my own past."

Whether designed as smokescreen or not, "Ballad of Your Puzzlement" is an excellent poem about the pitfalls of memory and the indelicacy of dramatizing oneself as either hero or villain. It has a parenthetical subtitle, which is not to be ignored: "How not to recognize yourself as what you think you are, when old and reviewing your life before death comes."

> Purge soul for the guest awaited.
> Let floor be swept, and let
> The walls be well garlanded.
>
> Put your lands and recollections
> In order, before that hour,
> For you, alas, are only
>
> Recollections, but recollections
> Like a movie film gone silent,
> With a hero strange to you
>
> And a plot you can't understand.
> His face changes as you look.
> He picks the scab of his heart.

The poem considers a number of metaphorical roles for dramatizing the self: as a tightrope walker on "the fated/ And human highwire of lies"; as a fly struggling on flypaper; as a murderer, presumably killing the one he loves, "She falls, and he bursts into tears"; as a hero kneeling at prayer; as a compassionate old man giving his

last dollar to a loathsome beggar; as a Chaplinesque
figure defying an indifferent universe. He asks ". . . how
many lives have you lived? . . . It is hard to choose your
dream." Then he gives· himself the sage advice that
began the poem: ". . . try to pull yourself/Together. Let
floors be swept. Let walls be well garlanded." We may
assume that he is neither spilling his guts nor wallowing
in confession.

Which, indeed, he is not. Most of the poems that
follow stress the universal quality in certain of his
experiences or imaginings. "Auto-Da Fe," for instance,
though possibly arising from the nearness of death,
concerns that deathless controversy as to the relative
merits of body and soul. The speaker is arguing both
sides, actually, but seems to lend weight to the preference
for body.

> Beautiful the intricacy of body!
> Even when defective. But you have seen
> Beauty beyond such watchmaker's craft,
> For eyes unshutter in darkness to gleam out
> As though to embrace you in holiness.
>
> ". . . though I give my body to be burned,
> And have not . . ." You know the rest,
> And how the "I" is not the "body."
> At least, according to St. Paul's text.

The meditator considers the usual reductive epithets for
body, such as "a bag/Of excrement," but notes that it is
not "I" but "body" that screams in the flame. Thus,
presumably it is "body," not "I," that knows what the
"truth" is of human experience.

> That
> Is the pure language of body, purer
> Than even the cry, ecstatic, torn out
> At the crisis of body's entwinement. That voice
> From flame has a glory wilder than joy
> To resound forever in heart, mind
> And gut, with thrilled shock and soprano of Truth.

He then considers how "All history resounds with such/ Utterance—and stench of meat burned. . . ." He considers some of the historical evidence, from the drunken driver who piles into the overpass buttress to Joan of Arc. He supposes that most scream, though there are exceptions who refuse to the body that priority of attention. The implied argument does not reach a final conclusion in the matter.

Although most poems in *Being Here* are not closely connected, there is one set of seven poems under the general title "Synonyms." Most of these celebrate specific instances of natural beauty, with one longer episode, a street scene in a city tenement district, showing some of its ugliness, but with the same reverence for life and beauty showing up in the most unlikely places. A kitten has been thrown into a great garbage grinder, but manages to scrabble out in spite of one or two broken legs. A garbage worker laughs and swings the kitten around by its tail. But a "grubby old dame" with a sore foot brings her cane down painfully on the man's wrist, gathers the wounded kitten into her apron, and hobbles painfully up the steps of her tenement. A drunk invokes God's wrath on the torturer, and the keeper of a little vegetable stall polishes apples one after another. The speaker, in a short final verse, concludes that "beauty is one word for reality."

Some of the themes explored in *Being Here* show up in a different form in *Rumor Verified: Poems 1979–1980*. "Convergence," for instance, is another encounter between a boy and a down-and-outer, reminiscent, though not so complex, of "Recollection in Upper Ontario, from Long Before" and "Blackberry Winter." The fascination with caves, suggested in "Speleology" and elsewhere appears again in "Chthonian Revelation: A Myth." The setting this time is the Mediterranean, the persona has a female companion, and the symbolic overtones of the cave are ancient ones of mystic union with the earth mother, from which one is reborn in harmony with nature.

Indeed, the experience of nature permeates much of this poetry, as though the sheer beauty of the world were pressing ever harder upon the poet's need to express it. Yet "Sunset Scrupulously Observed" must admit man's presence as a part of the picture, with the vapor trail of a military jet "like a decisive chalk mark that disappears/In penetrating a drift of cloud . . ." The military plane, which might be considered a blemish on a bucolic scene, is not so discordant with nature's purposes. The jet determines the metaphor for five swifts that "blunt-bodied like/Five tiny attack planes, zip by in formation, . . ." The unspoken analogy between man's military pursuits and nature's other predatory creatures is subtly implied with the sudden disappearance of a flycatcher first observed waiting for its prey at the top of a dying poplar. One of the swifts, which hovered momentarily at the tree to snap up the smaller predator, is quickly gone again "to fulfill his unseeable and lethal/Obligations, alone."

The enigmatic persistence of violence, some functional and some utterly irrational and pointless, emerges in a number of poems. In "Going West," it is the shock of a pheasant exploding on the windshield, blotting out the sun with blood and mangled guts. A more philosophical, but no less brutal image is used in "Looking Northward, Aegeanward—Nestlings on Seacliff": the persona, who has climbed to a rocky ledge on the Mediterranean coastline, sees the nestlings straining up with beaks agape and imagines the bloody sacrifice of a king's son long ago, intended to placate the gods. Yet the erupting volcano was not appeased, ashes buried all, and cities sank beneath the sea, the nestlings, like the sacrificed child, expose their feeble necks—"that blind yearning lifeward."

As always, the mysteries of time and identity still struggle in the never-ending impulse to definition. The past becomes, in some ways, more abstract, a haunting presence, sometimes breaking through in vividly remem-

bered images: a wretched drunk freezing to death in a
Minneapolis snowstorm; the dying father with his secret
cancer, "as though he leaned/At a large mysterious bud/
To watch, hour by hour,/How at last it would divulge/A
beauty so long withheld . . . ," this with the memory of
three friends watching the bud of a century plant . . .
"straining against the weight/Of years. . . ." In "Nameless Thing" the mystery of the unknown self becomes
disembodied, a nightmare presence that stalks the
house after midnight. The persona, with poker upraised,
pursues the unwelcome intruder. At last, it is trapped in
the bathroom. "I snatched the door open, weapon up, and
yes, by God!—/But there I stood staring into a mirror."
"But how could I/Have been expected to recognize what I
am?" It is an effective and dramatic treatment of the
restless shadow-self, loaded with the nameless horrors of
a lifetime.

The title poem, "Rumor Verified," is an ironic
consideration of how he might change his own reality by
some gallant feat of imagination (". . . trying to
believe/That, orphaned, you grew up in poverty and
vision,") or uncharacteristic action ("pray with the sick,
kiss lepers") or otherwise change the past by sheer
strength of will. Even the nature of the rumor that has
been verified is ironic. One remembers "The Ballad of a
Sweet Dream of Peace," in which the rumor concerns the
coming of God, perhaps to mitigate the brutal eucharist of
nature where supernatural pigs, long since eaten, wait to
consume the hapless consumer of their flesh. But in this
poem the rumor verified is not that God, after all, exists
(which might also be sufficient motivation for changing
one's past), but that he himself is simply a man, "with a
man's dead reckoning,/Nothing more." "Dead reckoning," with its ambiguity of perhaps fatal miscalculation or
simply unsubstantiated guesses about what he ought or
ought not to have done, is the right term for the poet's wry
attempt to come to terms with his recalcitrant past.

We may be sure that Warren is not through writing poetry, no matter how often he has delved into his teeming memories. He seems to have an inexhaustible source of creativity and such a sure command of imagery, metaphor, and sound devices that whatever he writes is well crafted. One may suspect that he is saying the same thing he has said before, using different images, but he has made so many varied observations during his literary career that we do not mind the repetition. Another book of poems is probably, even now, "yearning lifeward."

Indeed, Warren has just published (April, 1983) another long poem, even as this volume is on the verge of going to the printer. *Chief Joseph of the Nez Perce* will probably reach a wider audience than most of Warren's poetry, since its subject matter is already popular. It may seem new and strange that Warren should leap from his accustomed meditations on the Southern past to a northwestern Indian war, but on closer inspection the shift in perspective is not so great after all. General Oliver Otis Howard, who led the campaign against Chief Joseph, had come from action in the Civil War and Chief Joseph has perhaps a clearer claim than the South to honor and integrity in defeat. At least his predicament seems less sullied by original sin and intrinsically more hopeless in the face of history. Thus, he stands as a singularly pure hero of lost causes, respected even by his opponents.

Quite aside from the familiar struggle to survive against the white man's encroachment on ancestral Indian lands, presumably protected by treaties, Chief Joseph's private motivations are timeless ones, familiar to readers of Warren's poetry and fiction: the search for manhood to be worthy of his father, "whose eyes see all, and judge." The white men who pursue Chief Joseph have lesser motivations—revenge in the case of Colonel Sturgis, whose son had died with Custer, ambition in the case of Colonel Nelson Appleton Miles (a "glory-chaser," according to Major Lewis Merrill). General Howard, though humiliated by his treatment in the press, as Joseph's rag-tag band repeatedly outwitted him, conquered his own ambition to wipe out the taint of his seeming ineptitude and allowed Colonel Miles to receive Joseph's surrender. Miles did get to Joseph first, though General Howard, who arrived before the surrender, outranked him and could have taken credit for it.

With all the irony of art and life, the seemingly less worthy Colonel Miles offered Joseph quite generous terms of surrender and, even more surprisingly, tried his best later to see that those promises of a home in the West were kept. That Joseph and his people languished for a long time in an abominably unhealthy area of confinement in Kansas is not attributed to Miles or General Howard either, but to bigger luminaries, such as General Sherman, that hated scourge of the South, and President Grant.

The poem bears some resemblance in technique to Warren's earlier treatment of Audubon, though this is a much more sustained and closely integrated narrative. It is punctuated, however, like parts of the Audubon poem, by direct quotes from historical characters—not just Chief Joseph himself, but others from all levels of involvement in the tragic events of that era. Thus, the poetry sings a somber, but sometimes lovely, accompaniment to history, inspiring tears, perhaps, yet carefully avoiding an appeal to easy sentimentality.

The very "uselessness" of this war seems to elevate it to mythical status as indicative of each man's struggle to be worthy of the mysterious gift of life. The pristine status of Chief Joseph's central quest gains luster from the compromised state of the "civilized" white community—the greed of gold seekers, for instance, that made any attempt to limit western expansion into Indian territory quite futile and even induced some Indians, but not Joseph's father, to sell the land of their ancestors. After his defeat, even Joseph himself, whose tribe had never scalped a white man, seems ironically tainted by the company he keeps, such as the white man's hero, Buffalo Bill Cody, who once scalped an Indian and sent the prize to his wife as a gift. Warren speaks with quiet contempt of Buffalo Bill, who transformed "the blood of history into red ketchup/A favorite American condiment." Chief Joseph, like all survivors who outlive the moment of their greatness, must die in the world of contingency and compromise.

Warren has sought to reconcile some of the most contradictory elements in American intellectual life, particularly our inheritance of eighteenth-century optimism about man's goodness and social progress, with the darker, romantic consciousness of good and evil advanced by writers such as Hawthorne and Melville. Although he may lean heavily on the symbolism and imagery of romanticism, he does so with an irony and self-consciousness that recognize illusion and myth as a necessary part of the human frame of mind. Truth seems best expressed in paradoxes, such as those he defines in *Brother to Dragons*:

> The recognition of complicity is the beginning of innocence.
> The recognition of necessity is the beginning of freedom.
> The recognition of the direction of fulfillment is the death of the self.
> And the death of the self is the beginning of selfhood.

Like all mystical and paradoxical pronouncements, these sentiments are difficult to express in purely logical prose. But Warren believes that the self is not synonymous with the Faustian ego alone but must include irrational elements of the subconscious, through which the individual is bound to all humanity and to nature.

He has faced the existential meaninglessness of the world that moved Hemingway to rewrite the Lord's Prayer with "nada" replacing all religious terms. But for

Warren the answer to "nada" is not the Hemingway code
of the hunter, soldier, or bullfighter but the bonds of love
and obligation, particularly between parents and children
but extending beyond this relationship to a complex web
of being.

Notes

1. THE SOUND REALITY MAKES: BIOGRAPHICAL SKETCH

1. An unrehearsed interview with Richard Warrington Baldwin Lewis for the RPW Oral History Project. The interview was conducted by Susan Emily Allen at the Carolina Hotel in Chapel Hill, North Carolina, on March 22, 1978.
2. An unrehearsed interview with Robert Penn Warren for the RPW Oral History Project. The interview was conducted by David Farrell at Hotel Algonquin, New York, May 9, 1978.
3. "Robert Penn Warren Reflects on Kentucky Childhood," in *Lexington Herald*, March 11, 1977. A copy may be found in the RPW collection at the King Library of the University of Kentucky.
4. Interview with Warren, op. cit., May 9, 1978.
5. Ibid.
6. *Lexington Herald*, op. cit.
7. Steve Oney, "A Southern Voice," in *The Atlanta Journal and Constitution Magazine*, Sept. 16, 1979, p. 15.
8. An unrehearsed interview with Robert Penn Warren for the RPW Oral History Project. The interview was conducted by David Farrell at Fairfield, Conn., Jan. 25, 1979.
9. 24 May, 1924, DDC, File 12, quoted in Marshall Walker, *Robert Penn Warren: A Vision Earned* (Scotland: Barnes & Noble Import Division of Harper & Row Publishers, Inc., 1979), p. 54.
10. Ibid.
11. Ibid., p. 55.

12. Steve Oney, op. cit., p. 15.

13. Charles H. Bohner, *Robert Penn Warren* (New York: Twayne Publishers, Inc., 1964), p. 24.

14. *The Princeton University Library Chronicle*, III (April, 1942), p. 79.

15. Allen Tate, "The Fugitives" in *The Princeton University Library Chronicle*, III, (April, 1942), p. 79.

16. Ibid., pp. 81–82. Warren was almost twenty in 1925, so Tate's remembrance either of the date or of Warren's age must be in error.

17. Ibid., p. 82.

18. Ibid.

19. Henry Thomas Buckle, *History of Civilization in England* (New York: D. Appleton, 1970), p. 29.

20. An unrehearsed interview with Robert Penn Warren for the RPW Oral History Project. The interview was conducted by David Farrell at Fairfield, Conn., October 6, 1977.

21. Lewis D. Rubin, Jr. *The Faraway Country* (Seattle: University of Washington Press, 1963), p. 159.

22. Robert Penn Warren, *"All the King's Men*: The Matrix of Experience" in John Lewis Longley's *Robert Penn Warren: A Collection of Critical Essays* (New York: University Press, 1965), p. 76.

23. Ibid., pp. 79–80.

24. Ibid., p. 75.

25. John Lewis Longley, "Robert Penn Warren: American Man of Letters" in *Arts and Sciences*, Spring 1965. p. 16.

26. Cleanth Brooks, "Forty Years of Understanding Poetry," address before the 1979 College English Association Meeting, printed in *The CEA Forum*, Vol. No. 4 (Spring 1980), p. 5.

27. Ibid., p. 6.

28. Ibid., p. 7.

29. Ibid., p. 8.

30. Ibid.

31. Ibid.

32. Interview with Warren, op. cit., Oct. 6, 1977.

33. Ibid.

34. Ibid.

35. An unrehearsed interview with Mary O'Connor for the RPW Oral History Project. The interview was conducted by David Farrell in Davis, California, August 3, 1978.
36. Interview with Warren, op. cit., October 6, 1977.
37. Interview with Mary O'Connor, op. cit., August 3, 1978.
38. Robert Penn Warren, "Sirocco" in *Selected Poems 1923-1975* (New York: Random House, 1976), p. 219.
39. Eleanor Clark, *Eyes, Etc. A Memoir* (New York: Pantheon Books, 1977).
40. Steve Oney, op. cit., p. 52.
41. Eleanor Clark, op. cit., p. 169.
42. Interview with Mary O'Connor, op. cit.
43. In *Literature in Critical Perspectives*, ed. Walter K. Gordon (New York: Appleton-Century-Crofts, 1968), pp. 515–525.
44. Ibid., p. 519.
45. Ibid.
46. Ibid., p. 518.

2. LIVING IN TIME: EXPLORATIONS, 1923–1943

1. Leonard Casper, *Robert Penn Warren: The Dark and Bloody Ground* (Seattle: University of Washington Press, 1960), p. 88.
2. Private Porsum was inspired by the World War I hero, Sergeant York, whom Warren had met and read about.
3. Marshall Walker, *Robert Penn Warren: A Vision Earned* (Scotland: Barnes & Noble Import Division of Harper & Row Publishers, Inc., 1979), p. 249.
4. Casper, op. cit., pp. 115–116.
5. All references to poetry, except for *Brother to Dragons* and the poetry discussed in the final chapter, derive from *Selected Poems 1923-1975*.
6. Victor Strandberg, *The Poetic Vision of Robert Penn Warren* (Lexington: The University Press of Kentucky, 1977), pp. 149–150.
7. Ibid., p. 149.

8. "Robert Penn Warren Reads from His Own Works," *Yale Series of Recorded Poets*, Carillon Records, New Haven, Connecticut.

9. An Address delivered on October 31, 1947, in connection with McGregor Room Seminars in Contemporary Poetry and Prose, sponsored by the schools of English of the University of Virginia. A copy of this address is in the RPW collection in the King Library at the University of Kentucky.

3. THE DREAM SEA OF IDEAS: PROSE PERIOD, 1944–1950

1. Malcolm Cowley, "Mr. Warren's New Novel Is His Longest and Richest" *New York Herald Tribune* (June 25, 1950).

2. Ibid.

3. Jose Ortega y Gasset, *Meditations on Quixote* (New York: W. W. Norton & Company, 1957, 1961), p. 139.

4. THE ONCE AND FUTURE SELF: POETRY, 1953–1975

1. Victor H. Strandberg, *The Poetic Vision of Robert Penn Warren*, p. 99.

2. Paul West, "Robert Penn Warren" in *American Writers*, vol. 4, ed. Leonard Ungar (New York: Charles Scribner's Sons, 1974) p. 245.

3. Recorded interview with David Farrell, Fairfield, Connecticut, October 6, 1977. Part of the RPW Oral History Project, University of Kentucky.

5. FROM MELODRAMA TO PASTORAL: LATER NOVELS

1. Suggested by Barnett Guttenberg, *Web of Being* (Nashville: Vanderbilt University Press, 1975), p. xi, referring to Jacques Maritain's *The Dream of Descartes*.

2. Leslie Fiedler, "Romance in the Operatic Manner," *New Republic* (Sept. 26, 1955), p. 29.

3. *The Cave* was suggested by an actual event, in 1925, when Floyd Collins became trapped in a passage in Sand Cave, Tennessee. See Charles Bohner, op. cit., p. 146, for a description of the historical circumstances.
4. Charles Bohner, p. 153.

6. THE PLACE HE'S COME TO

1. Carl Tucker, "Creators on Creating—Robert Penn Warren" *Saturday Review* (July 8, 1981), p. 38.
2. Ibid.
3. Richard H. King, *A Southern Renaissance: The Cultural Awakening of the American South*, 1930–1955 (New York, Oxford: Oxford University Press, 1980), p. 285.
4. Harold Bloom, *The Anxiety of Influence* (New York: Oxford University Press, 1973), pp. 64–65.

Bibliography

A. PRIMARY SOURCES

1. POETRY

Thirty-Six Poems. New York: The Alcestis Press, 1935.

Eleven Poems on the Same Theme. Norfolk, Conn.: New Directions, 1942.

Selected Poems, 1923–1943. New York: Harcourt, Brace, 1944.

Brother to Dragons, A Tale in Verse and Voices. New York: Random House, 1953.

Promises: Poems 1954–1956. New York: Random House, 1957.

You, Emperors, and Others: Poems 1957–1960. New York: Random House, 1960.

Selected Poems: New and Old, 1923–1966. New York: Random House, 1966.

Incarnations: Poems 1966–1968. New York: Random House, 1968.

Audubon: A Vision. New York: Random House, 1969.

Homage to Theodore Dreiser on the Centennial of His Birth. New York: Random House, 1971.

Or Else—Poem/Poems 1968–1974. New York: Random House, 1974.

Selected Poems: 1923–1975. New York: Random House, 1976.

Now and Then: Poems 1976–1978. New York: Random House, 1978.

Brother to Dragons: A New Version. New York: Random House, 1979.

Being Here: Poetry 1977–1980. New York: Random House, 1980.

Ballad of a Deep Dream of Peace. Texas: Pressworks, 1981. (With Bill Komodore.)

Rumor Verified: Poems 1979–1980. New York: Random House, 1981.

Chief Joseph of the Nez Perce. New York: Random House, 1983.

2. Plays

Proud Flesh. Unpublished, 1939. (First performed, 1946.)
"All the King's Men." Unpublished, 1947.
All the King's Men. New York: Random House, 1960.

3. Fiction

Night Rider. Boston: Houghton Mifflin, 1939.
At Heaven's Gate. New York: Harcourt, Brace, 1943.
All the King's Men. New York: Harcourt, Brace, 1946.
Blackberry Winter. A story illustrated by Wightman Williams. Cummington, Mass.: The Cummington Press, 1946.
The Circus in the Attic, and Other Stories. New York: Harcourt, Brace, 1947.
World Enough and Time. New York: Random House, 1950.
Band of Angels. New York: Random House, 1955.
The Cave. New York: Random House, 1959.
Wilderness: A Tale of the Civil War. New York: Random House, 1961.
Flood: A Romance of Our Time. New York: Random House, 1964.
Meet Me in the Green Glen. New York: Random House, 1971.
A Place to Come To. New York: Random House, 1977.

4. Nonfiction

John Brown: The Making of a Martyr. New York: Payson & Clarke, Ltd., 1929.
"The Briar Patch" in *I'll Take My Stand*, by Twelve Southerners. New York: Harper, 1930.
Segregation, the Inner Conflict in the South. New York: Random House, 1956.
Selected Essays. New York: Random House, 1958.
Remember the Alamo! (Landmark children's book.) New York: Random House, 1958.
The Gods of Mount Olympus. (Legacy children's book.) New York: Random House, 1959.

The Legacy of the Civil War: Meditations on the Centennial. New York: Random House, 1961.

Who Speaks for the Negro? New York: Random House, 1965.

A Plea in Mitigation: Modern Poetry and the End of an Era. Macon, Ga.: Wesleyan College, 1966. (Eugenia Dorothy Blount Lamar lecture).

Democracy and Poetry. Cambridge, Mass. and London: Harvard University Press, 1975.

"The Use of the Past," lead article in *A Time to Hear and Answer: Essays for the Bicentennial Season.* Tuscaloosa: University of Alabama Press, 1977.

5. TEXTBOOKS AND EDITING

An Approach to Literature: A Collection of Prose and Verse with Analyses and Discussions. Baton Rouge: Louisiana State University Press, 1936. (With Cleanth Brooks, Jr. and John Thibaut Purser.)

A Southern Harvest: Short Stories by Southern Writers. Boston: Houghton Mifflin Company, 1937. (Ed.)

Understanding Poetry: An Anthology for College Students. New York: Henry Holt, 1938. (Ed. with Cleanth Brooks, Jr.)

Understanding Fiction. New York: Appleton-Century Crofts, 1959. (Ed. with Cleanth Brooks, Jr.)

Modern Rhetoric. New York: Harcourt, Brace, 1949. (Ed. with Cleanth Brooks). Later issued as *Fundamentals of Good Writing: A Handbook of Modern Rhetoric.* New York: Harcourt, Brace, 1950.

An Anthology of Stories from the Southern Review. Baton Rouge: Louisiana State University Press, 1953. (Ed. with Cleanth Brooks.)

Short Story Masterpieces. New York: Dell Books, 1954. (Ed. with Albert Erskine.)

Six Centuries of Great Poetry. New York: Dell Publishing Company, 1955. (Ed. with Albert Erskine.)

Faulkner: A Collection of Critical Essays. Englewood Cliffs, N.J.: Prentice-Hall, 1966. (Ed.)

Randall Jarrell, 1914–1965. New York: Farrar, Straus & Giroux, 1967. (Ed. with Robert Lowell and Peter Taylor.)

American Literature: The Makers and the Making. New York: St. Martin's Press, 1973. (Ed. with R. W. B. Lewis.)

B. Selected Secondary Sources

Beebe, Maurice, and Field, L. A., eds. *Robert Penn Warren's All the King's Men: A Critical Handbook.* Belmont, Calif.: Wadsworth Publishing Company, Inc., 1966.

Bohner, Charles H. *Robert Penn Warren.* New York: Twayne Publishers, Inc., 1964.

Bradbury, John M. *The Fugitives: A Critical Account.* Chapel Hill: University of North Carolina Press, 1958. pp. 175–255, 283–387.

Brooks, Cleanth, Jr. *The Hidden God: Studies in Hemingway, Faulkner, Yeats, Eliot, and Warren.* New Haven and London: Yale University Press, 1963. pp. 98–127.

Carnegie Series in English, No. 3. *All the King's Men. A Symposium.* Pittsburgh: Carnegie Institute of Technology, 1957.

Casper, Leonard. *Robert Penn Warren: The Dark and Bloody Ground.* Seattle: University of Washington Press, 1960.

Cowan, Louise. *The Fugitive Group, A Literary History.* Baton Rouge: Louisiana State University Press, 1959.

Cowley, Malcolm, ed. *Writers at Work: The Paris Review Interview.* London: Secker and Warburg, 1958. pp. 165–186.

Fiedler, Leslie A. "Three Notes on Robert Penn Warren," in *No! In Thunder: Essays on Myth and Literature.* Boston: Beacon Press, 1960. pp. 119–133.

Gossett, Louise Y. *Violence in Recent Southern Fiction.* Durham, N.C.: Duke University Press, 1965. pp. 52–75.

Guttenberg, Barnett. *Web of Being.* Nashville: Vanderbilt University Press, 1975.

Justus, James H. *The Achievement of Robert Penn Warren.* Baton Rouge: Louisiana State University Press, 1981.

King, Richard H. *A Southern Renaissance: The Cultural Awakening of the American South, 1930–1955.* New York and Oxford: Oxford University Press, 1980. pp. 231–286.

Longley, John Lewis, Jr., ed. *Robert Penn Warren: Collection of Critical Essays.* New York University Press, 1965.

Moore, L. Hugh, Jr., *Robert Penn Warren and History*. The Hague and Paris: Mouton & Co. N.V., 1970.

Rubin, Louis D., Jr. *The Faraway Country: Writers of the Modern South*. Seattle: University of Washington Press, 1963. pp. 105–130, 155–161, 176–184.

Southworth, James G. *More Modern American Poets*. Oxford: Basil Blackwell, 1954. pp. 114–119.

Stewart, John L. *The Burden of Time: The Fugitive and Agrarians*. Princeton, N.J.: Princeton University Press, 1965. pp. 3–205, 427–542.

Strandberg, Victor. *The Poetic Vision of Robert Penn Warren*. Lexington: The University Press of Kentucky, 1977.

———. *A Colder Fire: The Poetry of Robert Penn Warren*. Lexington: The University Press of Kentucky, 1965.

Walker, Marshall. *Robert Penn Warren: A Vision Earned*. Glasgow, Scotland: Robert MacLehose and Company Limited. In the United States: Barnes & Noble Import Division of Harper & Row, 1979.

West, Paul. *Robert Penn Warren*. Minneapolis: University of Minnesota Press, 1964.

C. Bibliography

Huff, Mary Nance. *Robert Penn Warren: A Bibliography*. New York: David Lewis, 1968.

Index

*Complete list of titles in the series available from publisher
    on request.*